African American Attorneys In Hawaii

By Attorney Daphne Barbee-Wooten

Copyright© Daphne Barbee-Wooten,
Amen Rasta I. Production Enterprise,
1188 Bishop Street, Suite 1908, Honolulu, Hawaii 96813.
email:daphnebarbee@gmail.com

ISBN-13
978-0-9841228-3-7
ISBN-10
0984122834

First Edition: 2010
Second Printing: August 2011
Second Edition 2020
Cover photo and back photo by Daphne Barbee-Wooten

Layout and Formatting by Eien Design Studio LLC.

Published by PACIFIC RAVEN PRESS
P.O. Box 678, Ka`a`awa, HI 96730 USA
www.pacificravenpress.com
Email: pacificravenpress@gmail.com
Telephone : 808-288-1630 USA
Fax Number: 1-808-237-8974 USA

Published in the United States of America

Printed in USA.

PREFACE

Mason B. Allen was the first African-American acknowledged to have gained admission to a state bar. He passed the examination for the Maine bar in 1844, before the Civil War. Allen learned the law as almost all aspiring lawyers did in this period: he read it in the office of a beneficent private attorney while working as this attorney's clerk. Three years after Allen entered the Maine bar, the Governor of Massachusetts appointed him a justice of the peace, making Allen the first African-American Judge. However, the first African-American was not chosen for partnership in any major Massachusetts law firm until 1978.

Robert Morris became the second African-American lawyer in the country, and, in 1852, he became the second African-American judge when the Governor of Massachusetts appointed him to a county magistrate position, a more formal judicial position than justice of the peace.

African-Americans were still slaves during this period, and many people resisted the notion of African-Americans as free citizens - much less as lawyers and judges. There were many more famous black Abolitionists then, like Frederick Douglass, than black lawyers due to the race bias in American law and society.

Allen and Morris' achievements were just the beginning of a long transformation from the injustices of the color bar to justices and judges.

In 1865, John Swett Rock of Massachusetts, a former physician, became the first African-American lawyer admitted to practice before the U.S. Supreme Court. Rock had abandoned his medical practice to study law in 1861. He also became the first African- American to be invited to the floor of Congress.

In 1865, Jonathan Jasper Wright became the first African- American lawyer in Pennsylvania, and five years later, he became the first African-American to sit on any state supreme court when he served on the South Carolina Supreme Court until 1877.

The first African-American to practice in Honolulu was T. McCants Stewart in 1890. He helped draft a City Charter for Honolulu and represented all varieties of people in diverse Honolulu. After he left Honolulu, he became a Supreme Court Justice in Liberia. So he was the first African-American Supreme Court Justice.

His daughter, Carlotta Stewart, was the first African-American school principal in Honolulu and his son, also known as McCants Stewart, was one of the first black lawyers to practice law in Portland, Oregon and later the Bay area in California.

After Thurgood Marshall was appointed to the U.S. Supreme Court in August 1967, all subsequent African-American federal judges over the next ten years were appointed to U.S. District Court positions and not the higher Appeals Courts. This trend ended in 1977 when President Carter elevated Judge A. Leon Higginbotham, Jr. from the U.S. District Court for Pennsylvania, Eastern District, to the U.S. Court of Appeals for the Third Circuit.

In September 1992, when the Just The Beginning Foundation held its first Celebration of the Integration of the Federal Judiciary in Chicago, some attendees worried that the future might yield   a shrinking number of African-American Article III judges, particularly at the appellate level, as current judges left active service in the federal judiciary and fewer judges entered the ranks to replace them. Judge Harry Edwards of the U.S. Court of Appeals for the

D.C. Circuit said, "It's irrefutable that the number of appointments of African-Americans has gone down. The distressing thing is that the number of potentially qualified people has gone up." In his remarks to those assembled for the Just The Beginning celebration, Judge A. Leon Higginbotham also lamented this trend.

To truly appreciate the accomplishments of African-Americans in the federal judiciary, one need only look back a century ago to the U.S. Supreme Court's 8-1 decision in Plessy v. Ferguson, 163 U.S. 537 (1896), which condoned state-sponsored segregation. The sole dissenter in that case, Justice John Harlan, said with prescience:

"The destinies of the two races [African-American and White] in this country are indissolubly linked together and the interests of both require that the common government of all shall not permit the seeds of race hate to be planted under the sanction of law."

As Justice Thurgood Marshall remarked:

"African-American lawyers have played a unique role in American history. Imbued with respect for the rule of law and the responsibility that such belief engenders, these lawyers have used their legal training not only to be masterful technicians but to force the legal system to live up to its creed: the promise of equal justice under law."

With this background, the plight of African-Americans in Hawaii is a necessary link in the chain of African-American history. My wife, Attorney Daphne Barbee-Wooten, was the secretary of the African American Lawyers Association, as well as President, and has kept archives and documents which this book shares with you.

Attorney André S. Wooten
January 2010

DEDICATION

To my father, Attorney Dr. Lloyd A. Barbee and my father-in-law, Judge Charles Stokes for their wisdom, guidance and love, and to all African American attorneys practicing in the area of civil rights.

INTRODUCTION

African American, Black lawyers practiced law in the United States before the Civil War ended. Although the number of black lawyers is disproportionately low compared with white lawyers, the numbers are rising. Black lawyers have been instrumental in obtaining and securing equal rights under the U.S. Constitution. Black lawyers have a keen insight into civil rights violations because they are descendants of an unfair slavery system based upon skin color. Black lawyers who made their way to the Hawaiian Islands continued the civil rights struggle and through law, politics, government and other social acts. Their acts helped Hawaii have a more just and egalitarian legal system.

As an African American lawyer in Hawaii, I felt it was essential to document our contributions. I start with early beginnings, recognizing two African American lawyers, T. McCants Stewart and Dr. George Johnson, both of whom attained International, National and Local prominence in Hawaii.

After presenting early African American lawyers in Hawaii, this book showcases legal decisions and events affecting race discrimination in Hawaii as it pertains to African Americans. From the 1950's through the 1980's, African Americans were not always welcome in Hawaii. Many liquor establishments refused to serve Black military men and allow them into their establishments. Mayor Frank Fasi appointed Dr. John Edwards to the liquor commission in the 1980's. After this appointment, the Liquor Commission began to fine establishments who discriminated. In the late 1980's, the Civil Rights Commission of Hawaii was created. Several of its rulings dealt with discrimination against African Americans.

The African American Lawyers Association was formed after a prominent Hawaii Court Judge referred to an African American Bail Bondsman using the "n" word. The African American Lawyers Association (AALA) is still an active watchdog for civil rights and gives away scholarships to the youth for writing essays on civil rights. Some of the winning essays are presented. Minutes of the first meetings of

AALA are included along with brief sketches of African American lawyers in Hawaii and historical events they were involved. African American lawyers of Hawaii members are active with the National Bar Association, the largest organization of African American lawyers and Judges in the world.

In 2004, AALA members traveled with the NBA to South Africa, Botswana and Zimbabwe. In 2006, AALA members travelled to Ghana and met with the Ghana Supreme Court and other attorneys. We attended a CLE class about "slavery" in Ghana. In 2008, AALA travelled to Cuba, met with attorneys, Judges and Cuban dissidents at the American Intersection (Embassy). A travelogue of these trips are included as a celebration with returning to Africa, meeting, connecting and observing the African legal system in African countries.

This book is updated to include activities AALA was engaged in up through 2020.

Attorney Daphne Barbee-Wooten

Table Of Contents

CHAPTER I
Early Beginnings

**T. MCCANTS STEWART- First Black Lawyer in Hawaii
(1854-1923)**

Attorney T. McCants Stewart traveled to Hawaii in 1898 from New York. He was the first African American Attorney to practice law in the Hawaiian Islands. The Pacific Commercial Advertiser announced his arrival in the Islands on November 29, 1898:

Mr. T. McCants Stewart, Who is Highly Commended Will Remain in Honolulu

"T. McCants Stewart, a distinguished Afro-American, who is a thorough-going American, if there ever was one, has arrived in Honolulu and will remain to engage in the practice of his profession- that of the law He is a lawyer of character and ability, well fitted for any business connected with the ability of Justice."

From 1989 to 1905, he practiced law in Hawaii. He was the first attorney to practice in the newly created Hawaii federal court before Hawaii became a State. He lived in Kalihi, Oahu, with his second wife Alice Stewart, and daughters, Carlotta (from his first marriage), Anna, Gladys and Kapulani Stewart. His sons, McCants Stewart and Gilchrist Stewart (from his first marriage with Carlotte Harris Stewart) remained on the mainland. Both were attorneys. His oldest son, McCants Stewart, was the first black lawyer to practice in Portland, Oregon in the early 1900's. His daughter Carlotta Stewart enrolled in Oahu College (now known as Punahou High School) and graduated in the class of 1902. (Punahou School is where President Barack Obama attended high school) She remained in Hawaii and became the first black principal of a public school at Anahola, Kauai. She died on Oahu in 1957.

While in Hawaii, T. McCants Stewart represented Chinese clients who suffered from discrimination and expulsion in immigration cases. In the early 1900's there was discrimination against Chinese in Hawaii. During the late 1800s, the U.S. government passed the Chinese Exclusionary Act. In 1886 Hawaii passed a similar Chinese exclusionary act which stated: "No Chinese passenger shall be allowed to land in any port in the Hawaiian Kingdom." T. McCants Stewart protested strongly against the Act as race discrimination, a subject he knew well and experienced on the mainland.

T. McCants Stewart was a prominent lawyer, preacher, writer, and educator before arriving in Hawaii. He was born in Charleston, South Carolina, December 28, 1854. He attended Howard University and graduated from the University of South Carolina with a Bachelor of Art and Law Degree in 1875. After law school, he practiced in South Carolina before moving to New York where he made a name for himself as an excellent lawyer, writer and civil rights advocate. He returned to graduate school, obtaining a post graduate degree in Philosophy and Religion from Princeton (College) University in 1878. He lived in South Carolina, New York, London and Monrovia, Liberia.

From 1880 to 1882 he was the pastor of Bethel AME Church in Greenwich Village, New York City. He was also appointed to serve as a member of the Brooklyn Board of Education for six years where he used his position to press for the hiring of colored teachers in the public schools and for school integration. In 1891 Brooklyn became one of the few integrated school systems in the nation due to T. McCants Stewart's efforts.

He was friends with prominent African American leaders such as Frederick Douglass and Booker T. Washington. His written briefs can be read at the Frederick Douglass papers in the Library of Congress along with letters to and from Booker T. Washington. He debated with W.E.B. DuBois about referring to African Americans as colored or Negro rather than Afro-American. He felt that the term Afro American held more respect and referred to a continent rather than color. He preached black history and pride at his church and in various speeches such as the graduating class at Hampton Institute and Tuskegee Institute. He wrote that the Ethiopian race, from whom the modern Negro of African stock are undoubtedly descended, can claim as early a history as any living people on the fact of the earth and that the Africans led the way, and acted as the pioneers of mankind in the various untrodden fields of civilization.[1] He urged people to recognize and respect African's contributions to world civilization.

He wrote articles in the New York Freeman, an African American newspaper in New York. Indeed, he represented T. Thomas Fortune, the editor of the <u>New York Freeman</u> in a civil rights suit against the Tranor Hotel. The Tranor Hotel in New York City refused to serve T. Thomas Fortune because he was black. He was forcibly removed from its premises. T. McCants Stewart sued the Hotel for violating the Civil Rights Act of 1873, and an all white jury in New York returned a verdict in favor of Fortune awarding him significant money damages.

Mr. Stewart advocated repatriation to Africa. Walking his talk about repatriation to Africa, T. McCants Stewart moved to Liberia to assist in establishing a College in Monrovia Liberia. Liberia is located on the West coast of Africa and was colonized in 1822 by Abolitionists, organizations advocating the return of black slaves to Africa, former African American slaves and free African Americans. In 1844, the Republic of Liberia declared itself an independent country. Many African Americans who moved and settled there became leaders, scholars and created a legal system based upon the American Constitution, excluding slavery provisions. In Monrovia (named after United States President James Monroe) T. McCants Stewart taught at the College of Liberia from 1882 to 1885. From this experience he authored a well known book, Liberia: The Americo-African Republic which was a best seller at the 1900 World Fair in Paris, France. He left Liberia in 1898 to settle in Hawaii.

A written memorial for Chief Justice Judd in 1900 gives example Mr. Stewart's talents as a persuasive compassionate advocate for equal rights:

> May it please the court: Were I to follow my mind, I would not speak; but following the promptings of my heart, I arise to lay my tribute of respect upon the new made grave of our departed Chief Justice. When I came to these Islands in November 1898, I brought a letter of introduction to him from a relative, one of my best New York friends. When I came here to the late Chief Justice, no bailiff barred the way; no secretary took my card for an introduction. But without ceremony, and without let or hindrance, I immediately passed into the

presence of a man, who received me with cordiality; and who during the entire interview, treated me with such urbanity that, within a moment after I had met him, I forgot that I was in the presence of the Chief Justice of the Republic of Hawaii, and felt only that I was in the presence of a noble man and a splendid gentleman. I remember this incident, and it tends to illustrate his character: I went into his room after a lengthy argument in connection with the Chinese cases (the proceedings instituted to exclude those Chinese, who on their visit to China, had taken passes, and felt they were entitled to return to Hawaii under them). Immediately upon entering he said, "What do you think of it?" I was surprised by the question, and made no reply. Suddenly, bringing his fist down upon his table, he said, with an expression of indignation I shall never forget: *"To exclude them would be rank tyranny."* He was evidently in sympathy with the underdog in the fight

12 Haw. 435,436 (1900)

In Hawaii, Attorney Stewart wrote several briefs to the Hawaii Supreme Court. Some of these cases are Koloa Sugar Company v. Brown,[2] (lease termination), Haw. v. Li Shee,[3] (marriage by proxy is not valid proof of polygamy); Pilipo v. Scott, [4] (summary possession case) and Harris v. Cooper [5] (disqualified candidate allowed to remain on ballot).

In 1905 he left Hawaii for London and then returned to Liberia. In 1911, he became a Supreme Court Justice of Liberia. He was the first African American to become a Supreme Court Justice in the world, over sixty years before Thurgood Marshall was appointed to the United States Supreme Court in 1964. In Liberia, he drafted the first legal code for Liberian Justices and the Revised Statues of the Republic of Liberia, 1910-11.[6] In 1918, he left Liberia, after falling in political disfavor with the President of Liberia, whom he accused of taking bribes.

In T. McCants Stewart's later years, he lived in the Virgin Islands and was active in practicing law and politics. He died in St. Thomas, Virgin Islands in 1923, after catching pneumonia during a visit to New York. He lived an active adventurous life, part of it in Hawaii.

In the words of T. McCants Stewart "Happy is the man, who ...leaves such footprints on the sands of time that succeeding generations are safe in following them." [7]

GEORGE MARION JOHNSON, J.D., LLD (1900-1989).

Dr. George Marion Johnson moved to Honolulu, Hawaii in the 1970's with his wife Evelyn. He planned to retire, after a distinguished career as Dean of Howard Law School, Assistant Elective Secretary and Acting General Counsel of the Fair Employment Practices Committee in 1941-45 (precursor agency to the EEOC), Director of the Commission on Civil Rights (1957), co-founder of the University of Nigeria after independence in 1960's and Professor of Law Emeritus from the University of Michigan Law School. He served the public as a lawyer, educator and administrator in many important posts. After moving to Oahu, immediate retirement eluded him as he quickly embarked on another exciting important venture-the creation of a law school in Hawaii. He became acquainted with many prominent attorneys in town and joined forces with Hawaii Supreme Court Justice William Richardson and others to obtain legislative support for a law school at the Manoa campus- University of Hawaii. In 1973, the first law school in Hawaii opened for class.

Before the establishment of the University of Hawaii (UH) law school, all attorneys practicing in Hawaii had to obtain their legal education on the mainland. Many Hawaii students could not afford the travel costs to study law in the mainland. With the creation of the UH Law School, more Hawaiian and underrepresented minority students with Hawaii ties were able to study law, become lawyers and contribute to Hawaii society. Governor John Waihee, the first State Governor with Hawaiian blood, was in UH law school's first year class 1973.

After assisting in establishing a law school in Hawaii, Professor Johnson was offered and accepted the position of Preadmission to Law School Program Director in 1974. The Preadmission program was designed to assist in admission problems of Hawaii's cultural minorities and economically challenged who were underrepresented in the legal community. At the time he accepted and created this program, he was 74 years young. He taught the first Preadmission course at the Law School and formulated a curriculum to encourage students to succeed in law. In 1974, 10 out of 11 preadmission students went on to complete law school and became lawyers.

Attorney Douglas Crosier was in the first Preadmission program. Mr. Crosier was the Hawaii State Bar President in 2002. According to Mr. Crosier, Dr. Johnson inspired me to become interested in law as a tool for reform. I learned through him that it is possible to change the world to make it better. Mr. Crosier recalled Dr. Johnson teaching students about human rights aspect of law, such as the internment of Japanese Americans in World War II, Korematsu v. United States, [8] Brown v. Board of Education,[9] (desegregation of public school system) United States v. Nixon [10] (President must turn over tapes to Congress). He recalls Dr. Johnson encouraging students to overcome all obstacles. He told students about his time when he was the only black law student at Berkeley. Whenever he would ask or answer a question in class, white students would stomp their feet so his voice would not be heard. His stellar legal career left the feet stompers in the dust. Mr. Crosier noted that Dr. Johnson was his first mentor, an inspiration, who clearly articulated a philosophy and genuine belief of what a lawyer is all about, he exemplified the love of law. [11]

The preadmission law school program has grown since its inception by Dr. Johnson and is very successful. In 2002, the program was run by Christopher Ijima. According to Mr. Ijima, the preadmission program has an incredible success rate. Each year approximately 12 persons are admitted to the preadmission program with 95% graduating. The preadmission students come from many diverse cultural backgrounds, Hawaiian, Filipino, Vietnamese, Samoans, Pacific Islanders, African American, Hispanic, Disabled and other groups who have historically been underrepresented in the Hawaii Bar. In 1987- 1997 the preadmission program was run by Judy Weightman who mentored many a prospective lawyer in the tradition of Dr. Johnson. Preadmission students have become successful lawyers, Judges, President and Secretary of Hawaii State Bar Association, published law review articles and won awards for oral advocacy among other successes. A huge mahalo should be given to Dr. George Johnson for creating one of the most successful preadmission programs at an accredited U.S. law school. In the words of Professor Chris Ijima, George Johnson Achanged the face of the Hawaii Bar. He was instrumental in diversifying the Bar in Hawaii. [12]

Dr. Johnson also lectured at the University of Hawaii medical school on the legal aspects of medicine and served as a member of the Committee on Hawaii Medical Association.

Dr. Johnson died in 1987 at the age of 87, but his generous spirit lives on. He left an endowment of over $500,000.00 to benefit UH Law School and UH law students. The George M. and Evelyn Johnson Trust created scholarships for qualified and deserving students in need of financial assistance at the UH Law School. Between four to six financial scholarships are awarded each year, according to Dean Lawrence Foster. (Dean of the UH Law School from 1995 to 2003). In addition to scholarships for students, a visiting George M. and Evelyn Johnson chair was endowed by the trust to enable the law school to obtain a visiting law professor to teach at UH law school. Professors who taught at UH Law School as the Johnson chair include Tanya Banks (1994), William H. Rogers (1995), Sherri Burr (Fall of 1995), Dan Henderson (1999) and Alison Rieser (2000-01). Dr. Johnson's generous gift has contributed to the success of UH law school by providing financial and educational opportunities to people who might not otherwise have the option of attending law school.

Before coming to Hawaii and sharing his knowledge of law, Dr. Johnson's accomplishments were many. He wrote an autobiography The Making of a Liberal: The Autobiography of George M. Johnson which can be found in the Hamilton Library at the University of Hawaii. In his autobiography, he recounts that he decided to become a lawyer, after learning about the discriminatory treatment of Filipino farm hands in the San Joaquin Valley, California. Filipino workers were hired at lower rates as immigrants and kept in segregated housing from white workers. Because there were few Filipino women, the workers dated white women. Gangs of white men, wanting to keep race segregation and to commit race hate crimes, assaulted the farm hands and burned their living quarters.

This injustice motivated Johnson to become a lawyer so he could fight for civil rights and equality for everyone.

George Johnson obtained his law degree and LLD from the University of California- Berkeley in 1929. He was one of the first African American s to obtain this advanced degree. In 1938 he obtained a J.S.D. from the University of California Berkeley. His thesis was AState Taxation and the Commerce Clause. He began his legal career as a tax attorney and was the first African American hired as California State Assistant Tax Counsel in the 1930's.

He was recruited to teach at Howard University, a predominantly black law school in Washington D.C., and met many attorneys instrumental in the civil rights movement. He assisted writing important civil rights briefs to the U.S. Supreme Court such as Sweat v. Painter [13] (Supreme Court ordered black admitted into Texas law school), Shelly v. Kramer [14] (Supreme Court ruled that restrictive covenants in property discriminating on the basis of race is unconstitutional) and Brown v. Board of Education [15] (Supreme Court ordered desegregation of public schools).

He became Dean of Howard law school in 1946 until 1958. During his tenure he introduced tax courses at Howard, established the Howard Law Review Journal [16] and brought prominent professors to teach. He taught students who later excelled in law and politics, such as L. Douglas Wilder, Virginia's first black senator and later Virginia Governor, and Federal Judge Damen Keith of the Sixth Circuit, U.S. Court of Appeals. Professor Johnson was known for his generosity and assisted students by giving them money from his own pocket. [17]

In his autobiography, he recalled being questioned by Senators regarding his membership in the National Lawyers Guild during his appointment hearing for Fair Employment Practice Committee (FEPC). In the 1950's during the McCarthy era, the National Lawyers Guild was accused of being "communist, in part because it was integrated and advocated an end to segregation. He reminded Southern Senators that the American Bar Association and Federal Bar Association did not admit blacks until about 1953. In order to meet and network with other lawyers in a national association, he joined the National Lawyers Guild, the only integrated lawyers association during those years. He was appointed to the FEPC despite Southern democrats' senator's objections.

Dr. Johnson also served as Director of U.S. Commission on Civil Rights in 1957. While on the Commission, he investigated discrimination in voting. He held investigations on whey there were no black voters in Louisiana, even though blacks were over 50% of the voting age. During the 1950's in Louisiana, a prospective voter had to have signatures of two (2) registered voters before they could register to vote. The Commission made undisputed findings that eight former slaveholding southern states discriminated against blacks of voting age depriving them of their right to register and vote. The Commission recommended that Federal Registers be appointed in these states by President Eisenhower; but it was not until President Lyndon Baines Johnson signed the Voting Rights Act of 1965 that specific laws and remedies to prevent voter discrimination were implemented.

According to Dr. Johnson:

"Black Americans have begun to show their political strength, as evidenced by the election of Black Mayors in a number of large cities, including several in the South. Yet despite the considerable improvement in the statue of Black Americans nationwide, far too many of us are still so dependant economically that we are fearful of acting politically independent. I am pleased that as a member to the Civil Rights Commission, I helped to lay the foundation for the Voting Rights Act of 1965." [18]

Before assisting the establishment of the University of Hawaii Law School, Dr. Johnson developed and helped establish the University of Nigeria in 1960, the year of Nigeria's independence from Britain. It was a challenging experience. In Nigeria, he was affectionately called Ese an ena mire - which translated into English means the law giver. He served as Vice-Chancellor at the University during 1960-1964 in Nsukka, Nigeria. He served with Dr. Nnamedi Azikiwe, who later became President of Nigeria. During Dr.

Johnson's time, the University of Nigeria expanded it curriculum to include Arts, Education, Engineering, Law, Science and Social Studies. A Street in Nigeria is named "Dr. Johnson" in his honor. The Law School of Nigeria is located on Dr. Johnson Street, as well as the George M. Johnson Administration Building. [19]

Dr. Johnson lived his goal to advocate the application of legal controls to conflicts based upon racial differences between otherwise similar human beings.[20] Dr. George M. Johnson contributed much to Hawaii, the mainland and Africa. With his knowledge of law, skills as a teacher and litigator, he sought to ensure that equal rights and educational opportunities were extended to those who were historically disadvantaged, and that includes Hawaiians as well as blacks. He earned the title of the Law Giver.

GEORGE MARION JOHNSON
Director of Preadmission Program

CHAPTER II
Following the Footsteps:
Black Lawyers In Hawaii 1920 - 2009

After T. McCants Stewart's venture in Hawaii, two other black attorneys arrived in the Hawaiian Islands to practice law. One attorney, J. S. Nobles, was a graduate from Howard University and arrived to practice in Honolulu in 1901. Unfortunately he died one year later from Tuberculosis.[21]

Another attorney with connections to Tuskegee Institute and Booker T. Washington moved to Hawaii to practice law in 1902. His name was William F. Crockett. He arrived in Hawaii and practiced law on the island of Maui. He worked as a prosecutor for over 30 years.

His son, Wendell F. Crockett also became an attorney and a prosecutor in Maui. Wendell Crockett's career included politics. He became a Republican Territorial Senator in 1951- 1953, and he was later elected to the Maui County Board of Supervisors in1958. In1959, Governor William F. Quinn appointed Crockett as a Judge of the Second Circuit Court. He was the first African American Judge in the State of Hawaii. In 1961, Crockett left his judgeship due to mandatory age retirement requirements at the age of 70. He continued his involvement with politics and was elected to the Maui County Board of Supervisors again in 1963. He died May 17, 1977. His son, William Crockett, III, still practices law in Maui and was once married to Hawaii Governor Linda Lingle.

More African American Lawyers came to Hawaii to practice law during the 1960's-2009.

Audrey Fox Anderson came to Honolulu from New York City where she worked as a criminal defense attorney in 1968. She was educated at Howard University and Fordham University School of Law. In Hawaii, she practiced corporate and real estate law. She was politically active and ran for the State Senate in 1974. She did not win the election. However, she continued to be active in Honolulu and was the first President of the Waikiki Residents Association, a watchdog organization formed to protect Waikiki residents from over taxation, pollution and crime.[22]

Barbara Ratliff came to Honolulu in 1972 from California where she worked with Attorney Howard Moore Jr., who successfully defending Dr. Angela Davis against politically charged criminal offenses. After Angela Davis' acquittal and Barbara Ratliff's move to Hawaii, she recalls visiting the Punahou Carnival with Angela Davis. Barbara Ratliff practiced law in Hawaii from 1972 to 1977. She taught Black History at the University of Hawaii. She also worked in the Civil Rights Unit of Legal Services, on prison litigation. She enjoyed Hawaii, especially the people. "I got to know all kinds of ethnic groups in Hawaii. The mainland is not as open."[23] While in Hawaii, she was appointed by Mayor Frank Fasi to Chair the Commission on Status of Women. She moved back to California in 1977 where she works as a solo practitioner. She is litigating a case seeking reparations for descendants of slaves from private companies and the government.

Jerry I. Wilson arrived in Honolulu the mid 1970s from California. He became a member of the bar in 1977. After he arrived he applied for attorney positions and was interviewed by numerous law firms in Honolulu. Although his credentials were impressive, the interviewing lawyers told him they did not have any African American clients and therefore did not see the need to hire him. Undaunted, he opened his own successful law practice where a majority of his clients are not African American. He has been in practice in Honolulu for over 30 years and has gained a reputation as a dramatic effective litigator.

AALA former-President and Secretary Judge Sandra A. Simms came to Hawaii from Chicago, along her husband Henry (Hank) Simms. Henry, a United Airlines employee, felt Hawaii was an ideal place to live and raise children. After arriving in 1979, Sandra clerked for Hawaii Intermediate Court of Appeals Judge Yoshimi Hayashi. She then obtained a job with the Corporation Counsel City Attorneys office. There she advised Mayor Frank Fasi and the City Counsel of Honolulu about legal matters, including race discrimination at Waikiki nightclubs.

In 1992 Sandra A. Simms became the first African American female District Court Judge in Hawaii. She was appointed by Governor John Waihee to the First Circuit Court in 1995. Judge

Simms handled many controversial high publicity cases involving crimes. One case was State v. Shabazz[24], where three young African American men were charged with sex assault on a young woman. During the trial, the prosecuting attorney referred to the defendants' race (black man) and the complaining witness race (non black female) in his opening statement. The jury convicted two of the defendants of a lesser degree of sex assault which made them eligible for probation instead of jail. Judge Simms gave one of the defendants' probation instead of jail. The prosecutor became upset and publicly criticized Judge Simms in the media as being soft on "criminals". Cartoons, editorials, letters to the editor, and even Governor Cayetano, questioned her judicial abilities, merely because she provided a young man a chance to rehabilitate himself instead of throwing him in jail. AALA wrote a letter to Governor Cayetano, expressing its displeasure with his criticism and pointed out inequities in his remarks. The Governor never responded to AALA.

Two years later, the Hawaii Intermediate Court of Appeals reversed the guilty verdict because the prosecutor's reference to race was discriminatory and tainted the judicial process. "The Court ruled: (w)e discern a distinct and reasonable possibility that the prosecutor's references to race might have contributed to the convictions of Crawley and Shabazz."[25]

The Court relied on an earlier Hawaii Supreme Court case State v. Rogan,[26] wherein the prosecuting attorneys office similarly referred to a rape suspect as a black, military guy and remarked that it's every mother's nightmare to find her daughter with a black military guy on top of her. In State v.Rogan, the court ruled: Arguments that rely on racial, religious, ethnic, political, economic, or other prejudices of the jurors introduce into the trial elements of irrelevance and irrationality that cannot be tolerated.[27]

There was very little media coverage about the Intermediate Court of Appeals' reversal in State v. Shabazz and the admonishment not to use race as a means to prejudice the jury. There were no cartoons, editorials, letters to editors criticizing the prosecuting attorneys office for using race in a prohibited manner, nor did the Governor call for the resignation of the prosecutor or Intermediate Court of Appeals Judges for reversing the decision. Judge Simms was treated unfairly when compared to the ultimate decision by the Appellate Court and the erroneous assertion of race by the prosecutor's remarks to the jury.

Judge Simms handled the criticism with grace and wisdom. She continued her judicial tenure and did not let negative publicity affect her decisions. She said criticism comes with the territory of being a Judge" and made decisions based on facts before her, not public outcry or popular opinion.

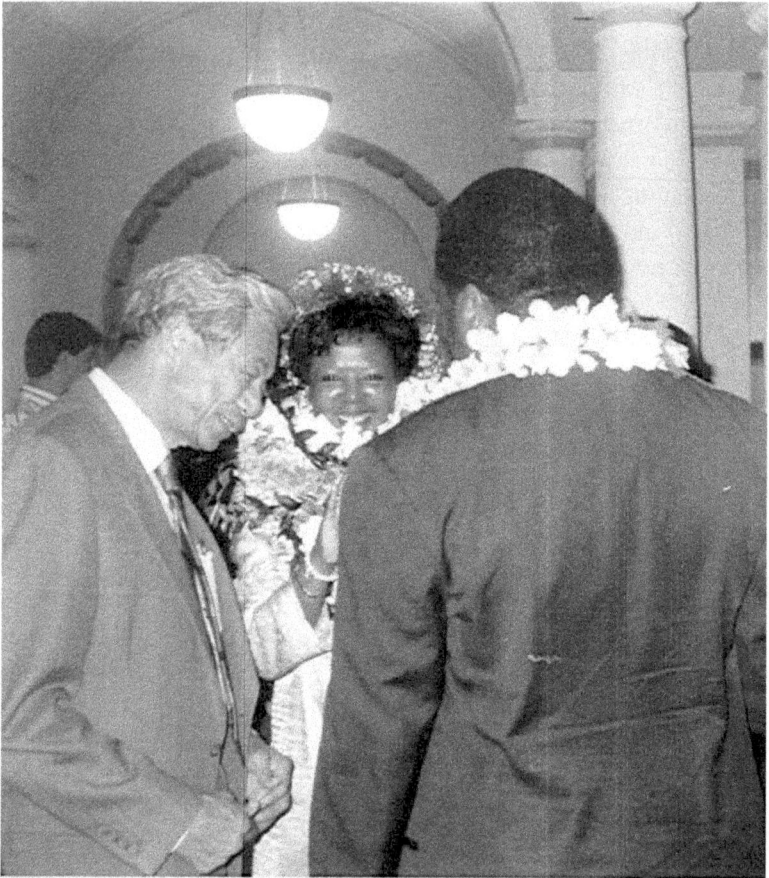

**(Chief Justice Richardson with Judge Simms at her
swearing in ceremony)**

Judge Simms retired in 2004 after she learned the Judicial Selection Commission would not retain her for another term. She was one out of several woman judges who were not retained by the Judicial Selection Commission, while male judges were routinely retained.

Despite Judge Simms' retirement in 2006, she actively participates with social organizations and the neighborhood boards. She is a member of the Sewjourner Truth Quilting club which designed quilts and pillow cases, is a renowned cook, and President of The Links, Inc., assisted in bringing programs such as the African Safari to the Honolulu Art Academy and in giving scholarships to college bound students.

AALA member and former President, William Harrison came to Hawaii from New York to study law at the newly opened University of Hawaii law school. In 1981 he opened his own law firm. His practice includes criminal defense, civil rights, civil litigation, personal injury and workers compensation. In addition to practicing law, William Harrison was active in politics and organizations. He was the first president of the African American Lawyers Association of Hawaii. (AALA) an organization which pushed successfully for the appointment of the first African American female judge in the State of Hawaii, Sandra Simms. He was appointed by Governor John Waihee to the Judicial Selection Commission and served for 6 years, 3 as Chair. He is active in Hawaii Association of Criminal Defense Lawyers (HACDL) and the ACLU. He is considered a top notch litigator in court and has successfully represented high profile clients.

AALA member Joseph (Joe) Mottl III was born and raised in Hawaii. He is the grandson of Noelle Smith, one of the first African American legislators in Hawaii during 1940s. Noelle Smith was a very outgoing civic minded politician who originated from Montana. Although he lived in Kalihi, Oahu, he kept in touch with the African-American community on the mainland by hosting notable African American travelers such as the famous poet Langston Hughes, who wrote about Noelle Smiths' family in his autobiography, *The Big Sea*.

Joe Mottl learned about politics in Hawaii first hand and it sparked his interest in law. Joe went to law school in California -Berkeley and returned to open his private practice office in Honolulu in 1982. He and his wife were among AALA members who attended the inauguration of President Barack Obama in 2009.

(Joe Mottl II with Judge Simms at the Hawaii Supreme Court)

Attorney Daphne E. Barbee-Wooten arrived in Hawaii in 1980 after law school at the University of Washington-Seattle. She clerked for U.S. Bankruptcy Judge Jon Chinen, and then worked as a Deputy State Public Defender. She was appointed Independent Counsel to the Grand Jury in 1985. She opened her own practice and litigated civil rights cases. She represented parents and students in the discriminatory yearbook cases against the (Department of Education) DOE. In 1988 she was appointed to the first Hawaii Civil Rights Commission by Governor John Waihee. She also became the first EEOC trial attorney in Hawaii in1988-2001 where she litigated class action civil rights cases in Saipan, Guam and Hawaii.

Daphne Barbee-Wooten was on the Hawaii Advisory Committee

for the U.S. Civil Rights Commission from 2006 through 2008. In 2009 the U.S. Advisory Commission tabled her membership under the guise that she criticized U.S. Supreme Court Justice Clarence Thomas and referred to him as an Uncle Tom in 2001. The U.S. Civil Rights Commission in 2009 was predominantly Bush appointees. There were inaccurate statements made by U.S. Commissioners that Ms. Barbee-Wooten was against Clarence Thomas because his wife was white. This is completely untrue as Ms. Barbee-Wooten's mother, Roudaba Davido is "white" and she agrees wholeheartedly with integration. The false allegations were similar to the far-fetched allegations that President Barack Obama was not born in the United States, when Hawaii was clearly a state in 1961.

Daphne Barbee-Wooten was a member of the Hawaii ACLU in 2001. She and the other two African American members, Faye Kennedy and Attorney Eric Ferrer, voted not to extend an invitation to Justice Clarence Thomas to an all expense junket in Hawaii. Some people erroneously felt Justice Thomas's first Amendment right to speak was curtailed. His decisions and rationales are anti civil rights and dismantle many victories that Justice Thurgood Marshall and Dr. Martin Luther King, Jr. fought during their lives. The ACLU eventually voted to invite Justice Thomas and he promptly rejected the invitation.

AALA member and former President, Andre' S. Wooten came to Hawaii in 1980. He graduated from the University of Washington Law School in Seattle in 1975 and briefly practiced law as a city prosecutor for King County. His father, Howard A. Wooten, was a Tuskegee flyer. Howard Wooten's photograph is on many posters and jackets as an icon of Tuskegee flyers. Andre' Wooten's step father, Charles Stokes was a respected lawyer, legislator and Judge in Seattle, Washington. His mother Josephine Stokes was a public school librarian. Venturing from the rain to the sun, Andre' developed a love for surfing. During his first five years in Hawaii, he did not practice law; he was an investigator for the State welfare department. He later took the bar exam and began practicing in Hawaii in 1985. He was past president of AALA, African American

Association of Hawaii. He produces video tapes about African history and lectures at the University of Hawaii on Black history, and other educational and civic facilities in Hawaii. He is co-owner of Amen Rasta I Production Enterprise- a video production company. He is married to Daphne Barbee-Wooten.

In December 2002, Attorney Wooten successfully litigated and won the largest civil rights verdict for an African American in Hawaii. A jury awarded Mr. Umar Rahsaan, an African American teacher, $1,055,000.00 (one million fifty-five thousand dollars) for race discrimination by the DOE when it refused to allow him to teach social studies classes. A younger less experienced Asian American woman was selected by the DOE, bypassing the more qualified African American male.[28]

AALA member and past President Rustam A. Barbee traveled to Hawaii from Wisconsin to become a federal deputy public defender in 1989. His father Attorney Dr. Lloyd A. Barbee was a respected well known civil rights attorney and legislator in Wisconsin. His mother, Roudaba Davido, was a nurse who graduated from the University of Hawaii nursing school. Rustam moved to Hawaii, leaving ice and snow and a job as a Wisconsin prosecutor. In Hawaii he worked for the federal public defender's office and handled many high profile trials. He opened his own private practice in 1997 specializing in bankruptcy and criminal defense. He was past president of AALA and was a member of the Disciplinary Board for Attorneys in Hawaii.

Darwell Leon Fortson Sr. came to Hawaii from California in the 1980's. In California, he was Director of the Neighborhood Youth Project of Los Angeles, providing food, clothing and housing for inner city youth. While in Hawaii he monitored and ensured diversity and affirmative action in employment. As director of the U.S. Office of Contract Compliance in Hawaii, during the late 1980's and 1990's he ensured employers followed the Civil Rights Act and did not practice discrimination. Armed with the threat of taking away federal funds from employers who discriminate, Leon Fortson was low profile yet highly effective. He organized mandatory training classes for employers that impressed upon them the importance of the civil rights act. When one employer fired all of its disabled employees, he ordered them to rehire disabled employees under threat of losing federal funds, and within days, the employees got their jobs back. He ordered the University of Hawaii to establish an African American Task force to document study and implement an affirmative action plan to hire and retain black professors and to keep statistics on black employees and students. Sadly, on November 24, 1995, Leon Fortson died in Honolulu. Fortunately, for the short time he was in Hawaii, he made employers realize the importance and benefits of a diverse workplace and effectively ensured that federal funds will not be given to employers who discriminate.

Professor Danielle Conway-Jones began teaching Intellectual Property, Contracts, Internet law and policy at the University of Hawaii Law School in 2000. She received her law degree, *cum laude*, from Howard University and has a master of laws degree in Environmental law and government procurement law from George Washington University law School. She lectured throughout Asia, China, Mongolia, Palau, Saipan and Guam. She was inspired to become a lawyer by her mother, Gwendolyn Conway, who was elected a Municipal Court Judge in Pennsylvania. Her mother's hard work and dedication to the law influenced her to become an outstanding legal scholar. Her former husband, Christopher Jones, was an attorney and worked as the deputy director of the Hawaii Civil Rights Commission in 2002-2007.

Professor Maxine Burkett teaches environmental law at the University Of Hawaii School Of Law. She is the Director of the Center for Island Climate Adaptation and Policy and attended the United Nations Climate Change Conference in Copenhagen in 2009. She is focused on "Climate Justice" and the disparate impact climate change has on poor and of color communities.

Mark Valencia is an attorney in private practice. He was appointed to the Hawaii Civil Rights Commission by Governor Linda Lingle in 2007. Mr. Valencia is an adjunct professor at Hawaii Pacific University and a certified personal trainer. He is also on the

Kuakini Medical Center Ethics Committee.

Shana Peete is an attorney in private practice. She and her husband left Memphis, Tennessee to live in Hawaii where they envisioned multi-culturalism as the norm in paradise. Ms. Peete's father was an attorney in Memphis, Tennessee. She is an accomplished athlete and tennis player/coach. She is also a professional model. She began to work in the prosecuting attorney's office and now has her own practice emphasizing on sports and entertainment law. Ms. Peete was elected President of the African American Lawyers Association in 2008. She, along with Joe Mottl III, Daphne Barbee-Wooten and Andre Wooten traveled to see the inauguration of President Barack Obama in 2009.

Gene Bridges was an attorney who was a Unitarian church minister. He marched with Dr. Martin Luther King, Jr. in civil rights marches in Selma, Alabama. He was a peace activist and could give a speech at the drop of a hat. He gave religious sanctuary to persons who disagreed with the war in Vietnam. He often bragged that he was the recycling attorney. As a minister he could marry people, he also had a bed and breakfast where people could stay for their honeymoon, as a lawyer he could divorce couples, and he also bred dogs which he would give to divorced couples as comfort. Gene Bridges passed away in 2007. Less than one week before he passes away, he was seen driving his car with a big sign "Impeach Bush. No More War" in Honolulu. An activist until the end.

Eric Ferrer is an attorney in private practice in Maui. He was formerly a partner with Attorney Johnnie Cochran in California. He left the high profile practice for a quieter serene lifestyle.

Paula Harris-White was an attorney who moved to Hawaii in the 1980's. She and her husband Ron founded the Hawaii Women's Business Directory and African American News. They moved back to the mainland in the 1990's.

Beverly Wilcox is an attorney from Tennessee. She moved to Hawaii with her husband, Dr. Carver Wilcox, a dermatologist. Although Beverly does not practice law, she was active with AALA and contributed to the award ceremonies for Essay winners.

Attorney Reginald Harris practices law in a major law firm. He moved to Hawaii in the 2001. Attorney Greg McClinton worked for the EEOC in Honolulu since 2006. He litigates cases in Federal Court. Attorney Seth Harris is a graduate from the UH School of Law. Seth Harris practices family law at a law firm in Kailua, Oahu. Not all black lawyers had success in Hawaii. Attorney George Parker III, a former deputy prosecuting attorney, made headlines in the 1990's after he was indicted by a federal grand jury for money laundering. His first mistake at trial was to represent himself. Another fatal mistake at trial was his waiver of a unanimous jury. A jury of 11 convicted him. One juror voted for acquittal. He made even bigger headlines when he walked away from the courthouse, tried to commit suicide by eating rat poison and ended up in a downtown alley where he was shot in the face with wooden bullets by Honolulu Police snipers who claim they mistook his cell phone for a gun. He was sentenced to 12 years federal imprisonment for accepting $10,000.00 from a drug dealer to represent him at trial. This was his first conviction. He previously was a respected deputy prosecuting attorney.

Johnnie Mae Sanders was a black female attorney. In 1998 she was appointed as a per diem (part-time) district court judge in Honolulu. She left Hawaii after one year of judgeship for unknown reasons and moved to the mainland.

Wendell Crutchfield, a former deputy prosecuting attorney left Hawaii after 2 years of private practice. He recalled having his bank records subpoenaed by the U.S. Attorneys office while he was representing a client in trial against the same U.S. Attorney. He was well liked and did not engage in unethical behavior.

Many African American lawyers practice in Hawaii moved away to further their careers. Attorney Karen McKinnie, who is also an actor and singer, moved to Japan in 1999 as an executive for Westlaw .While in Hawaii she worked for various attorneys and the State. She was secretary to AALA and hosted the African American Lawyer's show, "Law Talk" and "Legally Speaking". She subsequently returned to Hawaii in 2009.

Attorney Francis McIntyre who was originally from Detroit, practiced bankruptcy and immigration law in Hawaii in the 1990's. She moved to Mexico to retire in 2000.

Wanda Pate Jones worked as an attorney in the NLRB in Honolulu from 1980's the 1990's. She also hosted a local television show, the Afro-Hawaii News. She moved from Honolulu to Virginia and was later selected as one of the most outstanding attorneys in federal government in 2000. She is presently the regional counsel for the NLRB in Colorado.

Wanda Pate Jones

Professor Sherri Burr continues to teach law in New Mexico School of Law and is a Professor of Africana Studies. She returns to Hawaii occasionally. While in Hawaii she produced a public access television show called Arts Talk in Hawaii. She authored a horn book on Arts and Entertainment law.

Attorney Sandra Donnell-Smith practiced briefly in Hawaii during the 1990's. Her husband a military officer was stationed at

Barber's Point.

Law Professor Charles "Chuck" Lawrence teaches at the University of Hawaii- Manoa. Charles Lawrence and his wife, Mari Matsuda co-authored the book,"We Won't Go Back", about the necessity and benefits of Affirmative Action. Both teach at the University of Hawaii and are highly regarded civil rights educators and speakers, who previously taught at Georgetown law school. His wife Mari Matsuda is also a law professor and civil rights advocate. Other African American lawyers practiced law in the 1980 and 1990s. The following is a list of these attorneys: Solomon Johnson, retired attorney from California, Allison Jacobs, private practice, James Paige, (1988) Attorney Generals office, Pamela Boyd, deputy public defender and Hawaii Civil Rights attorney and former AALA secretary, Travis Stephens, (1987) deputy public defender, Adrianne Sanders, (1989) former public defender, Donn Fudo (1988) deputy prosecuting attorney, Khaled Mujtabaa, (1989) private practice and Vice President of AALA, Victor James III, (1997) private practice, Eric Ferrier, (1997) private practice in Maui, Brian Bilberry (1999) private practice in Hawaii, Charles R. Brown (2001) private practice, and Charles "Chuck" Lawrence, (2008) Professor of Law at University of Hawaii. There may be more African American Lawyers in Hawaii not mentioned and surely more to come in the future.

CHAPTER III
African American Lawyers Association

The African American Lawyers Association of Hawaii (AALA) was formed in 1988. The organization was created after the well publicized comments made by Hawaii State Circuit Judge Robert Won Bae Chang when he referred to a black bail bondsman, Art Lee, as a N in the woodpile.[30] At the time these comments were made, Judge Chang was chief administrator judge for the criminal courts. In response, the African American Lawyers Association called for the appointment of an African American Judge. Four years later, after lobbying by AALA, Governor John Waihee appointed the first African American woman Judge in Hawaii, Sandra A. Simms. He also appointed Attorney William Harrison to the Judicial Selection Commission, the organization responsible for recommending lawyers for judgeship. AALA provided moral support for black attorneys and served as a watchdog organization against racism directed at African Americans in Hawaii.

Lily James, an African American artist in Hawaii, was contacted to come up with a logo for AALA. A'ala in Hawaiian means of royal roots. There is also a famous park in Chinatown called A'ala Park. Lily James came up with a concept of a tree with two scales to balance justice. Hence, the AALA logo came into being.

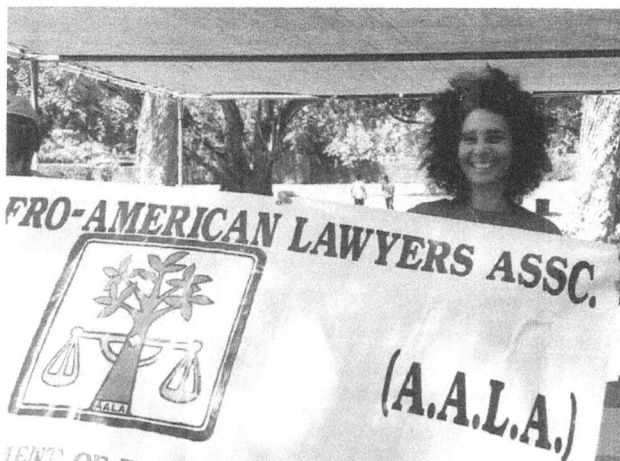

(The AALA banner)

The AALA bylaws were drafted and approved. It was decided that AALA should not be a non-profit organization, as we wanted to testify politically and have our viewpoint on the justice system known. The first meeting for AALA took place January 21, 1988 at Attorney William Harrison's office. AALA does not exclude members on the basis of race. Non-African American members such as Judy Weightman and Gene Bridges were strong contributors to AALA. As long as an AALA member is true to the principles of equal justice under the law and promoting the well being of African Americans and the law.

From 1988 to 1991, AALA was also instrumental in getting the Hawaii State Legislature to pass Martin Luther King Jr. holiday in 1991. AALA members lobbied State Senators and representatives who at first rejected celebrating Dr. King's holiday even though it was a federal holiday. Many legislators felt there were not enough blacks in Hawaii to justify the holiday. AALA pointed out that celebrating Dr. King's holiday was honoring civil rights, which is for everyone, not just blacks. Finally, after protests, lobbying, and a threatened tourist boycott, the State legislature agreed to make Martin Luther King, Jr.'s birthday a holiday in 1991. AALA marched in the Dr. King Parade to commemorate civil rights and Hawaii finally recognizing the holiday.

AALA filed a complaint against the Hawaii Department of Education (DOE) with the Office of Civil Rights (OCR), U.S. Dep't. Of Education in 1991 when a Kalaheo high school football coach told his team to get the (word), referring to an opposing team's football player. As a result of the complaint, the OCR ordered the Hawaii DOE to enact and implement rules against racial harassment in the schools in accordance with Title VI of the Civil Rights Act of 1964.[31]

In 1996 AALA filed another complaint with OCR based upon Kalaheo's High School yearbook, which contained a defamatory caption under three African American high school students photograph. The caption read: I like pig's feet! I like hog mallz! Where da colored green? Who got da chintlinz? The students had

won a talent contest and were not engaged in the act of eating or
talking about food. The caption was placed under their photographs
by a non African American student, and without their knowledge
or consent, merely because they were black. The caption held the
students up for ridicule and referred to the leftover foods eaten by
slaves during slavery days.

A civil rights and defamation lawsuit was filed against DOE
by Attorney Daphne Barbee-Wooten when it refused to recall the
yearbooks and to apologize for the racially insensitive and offensive
caption. The lawsuit, Sanders v. Knudsen,[32] settled with a public
apology by the yearbook teacher, $80,000.00 in monetary damages,
racial sensitivity training for yearbook advisers and clear rules and
regulations against racial discrimination in the public school system.
A year later in 1997, another public high school, Castle High,
published a yearbook with a photograph of a student in full Ku Klux
Klan (KKK) regalia. A non African American student, disliking his
teacher who was African American, wore the KKK outfit to class
and was photographed for the school yearbook. The principal
suspended him for wearing the outfit. After the yearbook was
published, the DOE and school officials claimed that the outfit was
that of a ghost or druid. However, the student wrote racist remarks
on his picture about lynching African Americans- something the
KKK would do. A discrimination lawsuit, Boyce v Knudsen[33] was
filed in federal district court. During a motion to dismiss hearing, U.
S. District Court Judge Susan Mollway dismissed the case stating
that there was no history of the KKK in Hawaii, and that therefore
plaintiffs could not prove intentional discrimination, even though
the African American teacher submitted an affidavit clearly stating
the discriminatory behavior of the student against blacks and DOE's
prior knowledge of his anti African American attitude. The case
was not appealed.

The next year in 1998, a young African American Junior high
student was called racial names and physically assaulted by non
Black students on Maui at Iao Intermediate School. The school
principal remarked that the problem of racism needed to be solved

by parents not the school. AALA and the ACLU filed a complaint to the DOE, who suspended the principal and ordered an investigation of the racial hostile environment at the school.[34] At the time this incident occurred, the National Bar Association (NBA), an organization of black lawyers and judges, was holding a conference in Maui. There were plans to donate a new top of the line computer to Iao School by the NBA. The donation school was changed to Waihee elementary school due to the remarks of the principal at Iao and a perception that race discrimination against black students was not being handled appropriately.

In the1980's through 2000, AALA played a principal role in bringing racism to a head and requiring Hawaii to acknowledge that there are prejudices against blacks in its midst which need to be rectified. AALA presented several public television shows on Olelo called Law Talk and Legally Speaking where AALA members discussed various aspects of law and its effect on people. AALA participated in volunteer legal services in conjunction with NAACP outreach in the community.

In the 1980's, many African Americans were discriminated against in nightclubs. One club, Spats, was infamous in its discriminatory tactics. Located in the Hyatt Regency in Waikiki, Spats would require African Americans to show numerous identification cards before allowing them entrance to the club. Non

Haneef Abdul Shafiq, Tim Riera, Rustam Barbee, Johnnie Cochran, Daphne Barbee-Wooten and Eric Ferrer pose with Atty. Cochran at ACLU speech in Honolulu.

African Americans were allowed entrance without identification. Mayor Frank Fasi appointed Dr. John Edwards, a prominent African American doctor, to the Honolulu Liquor commission. The Liquor Commission rules required that all establishments selling alcohol could not discriminate and stood to loose their license if found to be in violation with the anti discrimination rules. With Dr. Edwards at the helm, the Liquor Commission held hearings on discrimination complaints at the Waikiki nightclubs. In 1988, the Hyatt Regency settled the discrimination complaints before the Liquor Commission with a payment to the NAACP scholarship fund, a free evening at Spats in honor of Dr. Martin Luther King Jr. and agreement not to discriminate in the future.

AALA wrote letters of commendation to Dr. John Edwards, who was the Chairman of the City and County of Honolulu Liquor Commission in the 1980s. Dr. Edwards and the liquor commission were forerunners of civil rights in Honolulu. When bars in Waikiki refused to admit African American military men, the Honolulu Liquor Commission took the bars to task and under threat of having their liquor license revoked, the bars agreed to abide by civil rights laws and not discrimination in its admissions.

AALA wrote letters requesting that the speakers for its civil rights seminar, including Justice Thurgood Marshall and Federal District Court Judge Jack Tanner. Judge Tanner accepted AALA's invitation to speak at a civil rights seminar in 1991. Judge Jack Tanner's speech on civil rights was given at the conference at Ilikai Hotel.

AALA participated in the civil rights seminars and always made sure an African American lawyer was featured. In 1999, at an ACLU event, AALA cosponsored Attorney Johnnie Cochran, whose speech galvanized people to do more pro bono work for civil rights. He told the audience his favorite case was not OJ Simpson, but successfully obtaining the release of Geronimo Pratt from prison. Geronimo Pratt, former Black Panther was in prison for over 20 years for a crime he did not commit. Johnnie Cochran remained as his lawyer and eventually obtained freedom for Mr. Pratt.

In 2008, AALA invited Sir Dudley Thompson, Ambassador at Large from Jamaica, former attorney for Kwame Nkrumah (first President of Ghana) Jomo Kenyatta (first President of Kenya), and Bob Marley (reggae Jamaican superstar) to speak at the University of Hawaii. A luncheon was held in his honor. Sir Dudley Thompson was the Minister of Justice in Jamaica and is a well known authority on slavery reparations. He helped draft the United Nations declaration acknowledging slavery and the slave trade are crimes against humanity for which victims should have a right to seek just and adequate reparation or satisfaction.[35]

AALA continues to be a viable force in the State of Hawaii. In October 2008 when AALA testified against the head of the Hawaii Tourism Authority, who had racist and sexist emails on his computer at work. As a result of the testimony, Rex Johnson was given a severance package by the Hawaii Tourism Authority.

The next month, President Barack Obama, who comes from Honolulu, was elected as the first African American President. AALA President Shana Peete, Board of Governors Andre Wooten and Daphne Barbee-Wooten attended President Obama's Inauguration.

Shana Peete, Andre'Wooten, Daphne Barbee-Wooten at the Presidential Inaugaration for Barack Obama, January 2009.

CHAPTER IV
Hawaii Youth Essays on Civil Rights, AALA Contest Winners

Since 1991, the African American Lawyers Association has sponsored annual essays. The winners received money and a luncheon in their honor. In 1991 the first winner was Sarah Bremer. Her essay entitled "The Road to Freedom" is as follows.

Sarah Bremer: The Road to Freedom

Culturally diverse education is the cement needed to solidify the progressive foundation laid by the past generation of civil rights leaders. In the wise words of Martin Luther King Jr.:

Through education we seek to break down the spiritual barriers to integration; through legislation and court orders we seek to break down the physical barriers to integration. [1]

Thurgood Marshall helped crumble the legislative wall of segregation as the attorney in Brown v. the Board of Education of *Topeka*, Kansas in 1954 and in his subsequent career as the first Afro-American Supreme Court justice. Marshall's now vacant bench calls the next generation to continue building the path of equality. His legislative victories provided the cobblestones of this road, but, without the mortar of the mind to bind them together, it will never run smooth. The segregated curriculum of America's public schools obstructs the flow of spiritual integration and must be infused with the rich non-western cultures so that America's myriad complexions may coexist as peacefully as the colors of a rainbow.

If Africans, Asians, Europeans, Hispanics, men, and women are equal, then equal time should be devoted to the study of each of their histories and cultures. Not in America. western male culture absorbs a disproportionate amount of time in the American classroom. In fact, Compton's Encyclopedia, a popular academic reference, heads its civilization entry with "The Rise of Western Civilization." [2] This genre of unbalanced world perspective sends a distorted message of white superiority which cheats all students.

Superficial coverage of the heritages of minorities and women diminishes their significance and erodes the self-esteem of students of these underrepresented groups. While it is important to learn about foreign cultures, it is essential to study one's own past in order to better understand oneself.

A personal link to the subject matter may inspire a pupil to learn and provide him or her with positive role models.

Although it is less obvious, biased education also wrongs majority students. A hollow sense of cultural superiority impedes the development of a mature identity in today's pluralistic world. Ignorance of the valuable contributions made by all segments of society breeds fear and bigotry, whereas knowledge fosters appreciation and understanding.

Instead of emphasizing one civilization at the expense of others, a culturally heterogeneous program allows students to explore and compare diverse human experiences without stratifying them. A generation of multi-culturally educated Americans will pave King and Marshall's path of equality for all people.

[1] Coretta Scott King, ed., The words of Martin Luther King. Jr. (New York: Newmarket Press, 1983) 40.

[2] "Civilization," Compton's Encyclopedia, 1984 ed.

Front Row, Sarah Bremer and parents, back row, Daphne Barbee-Wooten, Sandra Donnell-Smith, Andre Wooten, Bill Harrison, Rustam Barbee.

There were many other winners of the essays, including Tonya McCoy, Alandria Fields, Tia Gross, Aaron Barbee, Ariane Harper and Kawaiarii Keaulana. Their essays are included. AALA seeks to stimulate and inspire young people in high school to think about becoming a lawyer and to think about the present, past and future of civil rights.

AALA essay winner Tonya McCoy at a luncheon with AALA members.

Tonya McCoy wrote about Affirmative Action.

What is affirmative action? When I first started the research for this essay I was surprised to find out over half of the people I asked didn't have a clue. Even the librarian gave me a puzzling unsure look. What was even more shocking was that I was clueless. Affirmative action is a policy that started 30 years ago to correct the effects of discrimination. It was created to give qualified minorities and women equal rights to education, business, and job opportunities. Under the Civil Rights Act of 1964 and the courts, the federal government requires that businesses and schools that receive federal aid to have affirmative action programs. Without these programs many women and minorities would not have reached the success they have. They would have either given up their dreams or failed in attempt to achieve them.

Affirmative Action has helped to create a society where all types of people from different ways of life have a chance to succeed. Women are now 43% of the students in law schools. The Banneker scholarship has allowed a very intelligent black man to attend a college he would have otherwise been unable to afford regularly. The percentage of blacks who have finished a four year college has quadrupled since 1950. A great number of blacks have moved up to the middle class. There are now more minorities owned businesses than ever. Affirmative Action set out to help women and minorities get ahead in life. Since its beginning other special interest groups have jumped on the bandwagon and turned affirmative action into a generalized preferential treatment program its original purpose has gone. Many fear that affirmative action is not so much about quality, as it was, but more about quantity. It-has been denied that affirmative action is just a synonym for quotas . Just the mention of it (the Q word) will send tempers flaring on both sides. On the side of the person filling the quotas because they like to believe they were chosen based on qualification. On the side of the employer/school because they want to believe they chose you based on qualifications too. Not all affirmative action programs are like this, and the ones that are will soon be disbanded. This is, one of the unfortunate consequences of affirmative action, many' minorities and women have no way of knowing whether they got where they are by their own efforts.

Racist is a word that has been used to describe the efforts of affirmative action. Just as racism has been an excuse for failure by minorities, affirmative action has become a blanket excuse for failure by white males. People feel it is reverse discrimination. However, there is little evidence to show it to be true. A great number of these claims are without ground. Some feel affirmative action has outlived its usefulness and putting an end to it will place more attention on individual achievement. While others say affirmative action still means affirmatively seeking out under represented qualified individuals.

Congress wants to change affirmative action to a need-based

policy, where it will not matter what sex or race, just as long as you re needy. They want this in order to create a colorblind society. It should not be abolished because it has not cured what it was meant to cure. One study after another has showed that discrimination in hiring words, giving scholarships, and handing out contracts still exist. If you substitute class for race you will bring a lot of people who are not minorities. Studies show there are more poor white people than any other race. This still does not address discrimination by race and gender. Without affirmative action there will not be a bright future for minorities. It would be a major setback in this country if we did not have affirmative action.

The attempt to end affirmative action, what is not being called the racial preference policy, will be a rough and long fight. It has been agreed that most mandatory racial preference programs will be disbanded before the year 2000. But even without these quotas some feel businesses will continue to hire minorities. A more ethical workplace makes more sense , said Thomas Sowell. Even if affirmative action ceased to exist, there are more than enough civil rights laws to keep people in line. Title VII of the 1964 Civil Rights Act lets you sue if you are discriminated against because of sex, origin, race, religion, or color. Then there is the Equal Pay Act of 1963, the Age Discrimination of Employment Act of 1967, and the Americans with Disabilities Act of 1990. Affirmative action will always continue to exist because each of these reflects in some way what was set out to achieve by affirmative action.

In conclusion to me affirmative action means more of an opportunity for my people and me to advance in life. To end it would be a problem in the efforts to motivate minorities to succeed. We need to better educate people on the diversity needed in colleges and businesses. Affirmative action creates this diversity.

1998 "Leon Fortsen" AALA*ESSAY WINNER-KAWAIARII KEAULANA

Kawaiarii Keaulana, a graduate from Kailua High School won the 1998 Leon Fortsen AALA essay. His winning essay follows:

Aloha and Hello!

My name is Kawaiarii Melia Virtua Keaulana and I am a eighteen year old student at the University of Hawaii at Manoa. My future goals and aspiration in life and are to attain a bachelor's degree in English Literature and a PhD in a secondary education. With these degrees I plan to help the youth of Hawaii attain higher education and help assist them in gaining the mindset that " They are somebody" I am recent graduate of Kailua high school and have attended He'eia Benjamin Parker, Blanch Pope, and Waimanalo elementary schools. These schools have helped contribute to my education in order to gain the knowledge and move on and become a successful college student.

I was born and raised in Hawaii (windward, Oahu) and have lived there for eighteen years. I was raised in both the Hawaiian and Tahitian lifestyles which have taught me a lot about racism. As a child I was exposed to the mindset that everyone had not been created equal do to my being Hawaiian and having been discriminated against in many ways. Within Hawaii's educational system it is widely known Hawaiian or part Hawaiian students do not prosper in education as well as the "White" or Anglo Saxon students. Hawaiian or part Hawaiian students are treated differently than white students.

One of the ways discrimination against these students is by depriving them from a "normal" education. Many programs have been started in education systems to "help" the students by separating them from their peers and containing them in class room on a one on one bases with a teacher. This style of teaching has not helped these students, but causes them to lack both the academic and social skills in order to excel in standardized tests.

Racism has always stood out within Hawaii's educational system. Kailua high school has many racial identity. Another form of racial discrimination at Kailua high school are the racial slurs that many students have written and verbally publicized.

Racism has also played a major role at the University of Hawaii at Monoa. There has been a controversy when a building named after a former professor who had been known to write a book quoting that "black students" or students of color should not receive the same privileges as the white students". Mr. Porteus is the professor the building was named after, whom had been alleged to have discriminated against students other than white students. Other forms of racial discrimination that have been overlooked at the University is the fact that foreign students are given a special dormitory called Hale Monoa. This dorm is only open to Foreign students and does not allow other students of other races to apply there.

Having to live in a place known as a "melting pot" has been a great experience for me as a person. I have had the experience of meeting many different people of many different races. Some forms of racial discrimination that are visible in Hawaii's community in the racial slurs, such as Haole (Caucasian), Kanak (Hawaiian), Jap (Japanese), Chang (Chinese) etc. These slurs have been instilled in Hawaiian youth for many years. Within the community in Hawaii I have personally learned to over look the fact of racial discrimination and judge a person on their qualities as a person and not their physical appearance. I feel that the people of Hawaii should "work together" to build a happy community without the racism.

Alandria Fields

Alandria Fields, AALA Essay Winner

Equality?

Before, during the civil rights movement, schools were segregated. That is, the whites went to one school and the blacks went to a different school. The black schools were a lot more inferior to the white schools in the same states. The books that went to the black schools were outdated and handed down books from the white schools. Sometimes there were pages missing from the books or graffiti written all over them. The schools by themselves were inefficient. There wasn't enough desks or any other supplies sufficient for the students in the black schools. The supplies that the black students did have were handed down materials from the white schools. You see, whenever the supplies from the white schools became no longer efficient enough to teach the white students, they were handed down to the black ones. The only proper education a black student could receive was that of private schools. Many black families however didn't have enough money to send their kids to one. It was during the civil rights movement and many blacks were denied the equal opportunities of work and school. So, consequently, many parents became angered at the fact that their kids could not receive a proper public education.

One man in particular became so angry at the fact that his daughter couldn't get a proper public school education that he decided to take a stand. His name was Oliver Brown and he decided to take his issue to the courts. His daughter Linda Brown went to an elementary school that was far away from her home. The white elementary school on the other hand was only several blocks away. Instead of putting his daughter at a school so far away, Oliver Brown decided to enroll his daughter into the white elementary school. The principal of the white school refused to do this because little Linda Brown was black. Nothing else was the matter with her besides the color of her skin, which she had no control over, and wasn't such a deal anyway.

Oliver Brown took his dilemma to McKinley Burnett, the head of Topeka's branch of the National Association for the Advancement of Colored People (NAACP). Burnett had wanted to challenge the segregation of public schools anyway, and he saw this case as his chance. So McKinley and Brown decided to make a case out of it.

Soon many other parents joined the bandwagon because they didn't really like the idea of segregated schools either. They also wanted the schools to be desegregated. The decision to try and desegregate the public schools sparked a lot of interest all over the United States.

Most whites didn't want their kids to intermingle with blacks at schools. I guess they thought if their kids spent too much time with blacks, they would start to like them. There were even some blacks that weren't too fond of the idea. They were scared and didn't want to spur up too much trouble. Most blacks wanted the desegregation to happen though. They were tired of having uneducated kids and having to live inferior to whites. Some whites even supported the desegregation of schools. Brown vs. Board of Education sparked so much controversy that it went all the way up to the Supreme Court. There was a lot of arguing and a lot of people were mad, but finally the Supreme Court gave in and declared the segregation of public schools Unconstitutional. That was a happy day for blacks everywhere. They finally found a way for everyday black kids everywhere to make something of their lives. They thought everything was over and education in the public school systems would finally be equal.

Equality though is something for a dream world. I don't think there will ever be true and pure equality on this earth. There never has been and I don't think there ever will be. This is why I think Brown vs. Board of Education desegregated schools but it didn't guarantee equality.

Nothing from the world is guaranteed. The only guarantee's I trust are the ones from God. Everyone is supposedly guaranteed free speech, the rights to fair trials and many other things found in the Constitution but a lot of those guarantees can and are broken every day. So just because Brown vs. Board of education "guarantees" equality doesn't mean that it actually exists. People have a natural tendency to be prejudice. Prejudice is only the thought that other people are different based on certain physical characteristics. For example, I can look at a black man and think he's incapable of writing an essay, and that will be prejudice. But when I actually deny him the right of writing it, and give his job to a white man, that's discrimination. I am denying him equal opportunities. Both prejudice and discrimination are equally bad. Prejudice leads to discrimination, and what people don't understand is that everyone is prejudice about something in at least one part of his or her lives. That's like telling a person not to judge others. I can try my best not to judge, but it's just the natural tendency for me and everyone else to do so. Just like it's the natural tendency to be prejudice.

* * *

There have been many other improvements in education since

the Brown vs. Board of Education decision. For one, it desegregated public schools all over America, thus making it possible for minorities to receive a much better education then what they had before. In the past, minorities, particularly blacks, were forced to get used books from the white kids that were outdated and inaccurate which caused them to learn the wrong things. They didn't have the proper utensils or classroom arrangements so the typical learning environment looked rather poorly. When the schools finally became desegregated, blacks were able to receive a much better education like their white counterparts.

Desegregating the schools also made it possible for blacks and whites to interact. The reason this was important was because there were a lot of stereotypes about the two different groups that needed to be squashed. Today, there are stereotypes about races that still need to be squashed. If I didn't attend school here in Hawaii with a variety of different cultures, I would probably go along with the popular stereotype that says all Chinese people are smart. I go to a desegregated school and know firsthand that this is merely a stereotype. This is why desegregation of schools is still helpful today.

In some places where there are still "one race" communities where the desegregation of schools showed no purpose. They still go to school with their own race. In many cities across the United States, a person could easily find a town where there is an unofficial "white" school and across the tracks there's an unofficial "black" school. There aren't any laws stating these things but the people just choose to stay within their own boundaries. I guess that's just the way they want things to happen.

I am really glad that the schools today are desegregated. I like intermingling with my White friends and Asian friends and also my very own Black friends. Through my experiences of attending desegregated schools, I have learned that it's not the color of a person that makes them worth knowing. It's what's in the inside. If I didn't go to a desegregated school, I might have never known this. America has made a lot of progress affecting the equal rights of its citizens. Compared to how things were before the civil rights movement, anyone who says we haven't made any progress has got their eyes closed. Still, a lot of improvements can still be made. At least America is trying.

Voting Rights Act by Arianne Harper

AALA's 2006 winner of the African American Essay Contest, Arianne Harper, wrote an excellent article about the Voting Rights. She was given money and a luncheon at Paliminos. Her essay, Voting Right Act follows.

The Voting Rights Act of 1965 was passed to guarantee that no federal, state or local government shall in any way impede or discourage people from voting or registering to vote because of their race or color. African Americans and other racial and ethnic minority Americans were actually guaranteed the right to vote by the 15th amendment to the U.S. Constitution passed in 1850. For nearly 100 years it was ignored and African-Americans lived through a long and infamous period of discriminatory and racist attitudes. States and local municipalities continued to use tactics such as poll taxes, literacy tests, and outright intimidation to stop people from casting free and unfettered ballots. Thus the Voting Rights Act of 1965 was set in place to insure that no government could legally impose any infringement to the voting process based on race or ethnicity. Now, over four decades later, sections of the act are set to expire. The looming expiration date, August 6, 2007, has ignited much debate.

The provisions' effectiveness, relevance, and extension are being challenged. Opponents to the act's renewal question whether the provisions remain relevant and effective in this day and age. Edward J. Blum, a visitor of the American Enterprise Institute, testified before a congressional committee recently that the provisions are outdated. "Bull Connor is dead", he said, referring to the notorious segregationalist police commissioner in Birmingham, AL, "and so is every Jim Crow-era segregationalist intent on keeping blacks from the polls. In 1965, Congress found "rampant racial discrimination" in Southern elections, he said. "By today however, the data simply do not support a similar finding." Or does it?

Hearings held in 2005 and 2006 have found a new generation of tactics, including annexations, at-large elections, last minute poll place changes, and disenfranchising redistricting practices which have had a discriminatory impact on voters. Racial and ethnic minority American voters have been affected the most. Extensive hearings in the House and Senate Judiciary Committees have proven that some states, local municipalities and jurisdictions have proven records of still trying to use official means to discourage racial and ethnic minority Americans from registering and voting. Long lines, flawed lists of ineligible voters, and faulty ballots are among the problems that plague the election process. These activities predominately occur in minority districts. The incidents were considered administrative glitches although they clearly had "racial overtones". These actions are illegal and unconstitutional. We need to renew, reauthorize, and restore the expiring provisions of the Voting Rights Act of 1965 to ensure that the discriminatory tactics that were so well-documented by the committee hearings are adequately addressed.

Statistics project that in the next 10 years, greater than 50% of the population of the United States will be " people of color." This suggests that the majority vote will be non-white. Given these projections, the practicality of losing the right to vote is not feasible. "It's a myth that we stand to lose the right to vote, but we do stand to lose critical protections that have allowed us to participate fully in the political process," said Debo Adegbile, associate director of litigation at the NAACP Legal Defense and Educational Fund. "We've seen consistently, even with the provisions in place, continuing efforts to weaken minority voices in the electoral process." The provisions also require interpreters and translated election materials in precincts with high populations of non-white voters who have difficulty understanding English, says Margaret Fung, executive director of the Asian American Legal defense and Education Fund.

The original Voting Rights Act of 1965 is considered one of our nation's most important civil rights laws. It was intended to guarantee the full realization of the 15th amendment to the Constitution . Most of the sections about to expire resulted from race based and violent tactics. It is evident that America is not yet free of a racism and discrimination against African Americans and people of color. It is important that we fight to keep this acts protection. We need to urge our representatives in the strongest terms possible to actively support the Fannie Lou Hammer, Rosa Parks and Coretta Scott King Voting Rights Act Reauthorization and Amendments Act of 2006 when it comes before them on the floor, and oppose any weakening amendments which may be offered. We, the youth of America must embrace our heritage and realize our place and power in the electoral process. We must embrace change, become active in leadership and civic duties to stem this tide. If we intend on keeping America "the land of the free", it is crucial that this act be renewed. The guarantee of full protection of all American voting rights must be realized in our nation, in this decade.

AALA members with Arianne Harper and her Mother.

All essay winners were given monetary contributions for their college education and feasted at a luncheon.

In addition to sponsoring the essay contest, AALA has a

speaker's bureau, and many members, including Judge Sandra Simms, Attorney Andre S. Wooten, Attorney Rustam A. Barbee, and Attorney Bill Harrison speak on various issues.

AALA sponsors yearly civil rights essays scholarship contests to encourage youth to educate themselves about the civil rights struggle.

CHAPTER V
Courts and Hawaii Civil Rights Commission Decisions Concerning African Americans Issues

The Hawaii State Constitution reads:

"No person shall be deprived of life, liberty, or property without due process of law, nor denied the equal protection of the laws, nor be denied the enjoyment of the person's civil rights or to be discriminated against and exercising therefore because of race, religion, sex, or ancestry." See Article 1, Section 5, Hawaii State Constitution.

When several Waikiki night clubs were discriminating against African American men, cases were brought before the Honolulu Liquor Commission in the 1970's. There was no Hawaii Civil Rights Commission at that time. In Hyatt, Corp. v. Honolulu Liquor Commission, 69 Haw. 238 (1987), the Hawaii Supreme Court reaffirmed "this expressed public policy against racial discrimination is beyond question." Id. at pg 244. In 1989, statutes were enacted to establish a Hawaii Civil Rights Commission to enforce the public policy against racial discrimination. See Chapter 489 Hawaii Revised Statutes. The law now specifically states,

"Unfair discriminatory practices which deny or attempt to deny a person's a full and equal enjoyment of goods, services, facilities, privileges, advantages and accommodations of places of public accommodation on the basis of race, sex, color, religion, ancestry, or disability are prohibited." See Section 489-3 Hawaii Revised Statutes.

There are similar statutes which prohibit discrimination on the basis of race, sex, religion, national origin, and sexual orientation in housing and in employment in Hawaii . In the 1980's more African Americans were living in Hawaii than previous years. While Hawaii is a multi-ethnic state, there is still discrimination on the basis of color, where the lighter skinned people were treated better than darker skinned people of all races, including Filipinos, Hawaiians, Japanese, Chinese, Samoans, and Puerto Ricans. This was part of the plantation mentality, which still lingered on. With the enactment of these new civil rights laws and the prosecution of these laws, citizens of Hawaii are now more aware of their rights against discrimination and to not tolerate discriminatory acts against them.

Two cases decided by Hawaii Appellate Courts, State v.Rogan, State v Shabazz, prohibit attorneys from using race in arguments to the jury to sway emotions and prejudices. Both cases involved black suspects charged with sex assault against a non black complainant. In State v. Batson,[36] the Hawaii Supreme Court followed the U.S. Supreme Court in ruling that attorneys may not make preemptory challenges of a prospective juror based upon race. In the words of the court:

"Whenever the prosecution exorcizes its preemptory challenges as to exclude entirely for the jury all persons who are of the same ethnic minority as the defendant, and that exclusion is challenged by the defense, there will be an inference that the exclusion was racially motivated, and the prosecutor must, to the satisfaction of the court, explain his or her challenges on a non-ethnic basis."[37]

In State v. Richie,[38] the Hawaii Supreme Court ruled that the lack of African Americans in a jury was grounds for reversal in a case involving a black man, charged with promoting prostitution for playing a boom box for women who engaged in a lap dance bachelor party on Kauai. The court noted there were few African Americans in Hawaii and that the fact there were no African Americans in the jury pool was not discriminatory. However, the Richie case is an example of selective prosecution because other establishments and organizations such as Chippendales (an all male dance review) and strip clubs where lap dancing occurs in Hawaii were not charged with prostitution. Richie, the lone black man was the first person arrested and convicted for promoting prostitution while the women who lap danced at the bachelor party were not convicted of prostitution. The lap dance bachelor party in Richie's case was requested by undercover police who targeted Mr. Richie.

The Hawaii Civil rights Commission (HCRC) addressed racial slurs of African Americans in two published decisions. In Smith v. MTL[39] a bus driver called an African American passenger "nigger" when a dispute arose regarding a bus stop. The HCRC ruled this was race discrimination in public accommodations and awarded the passenger $30,000.00 in damages.

In <u>White v. State of Hawaii, University of Hawaii and Wallace</u>,[40] the HCRC found discrimination after a student coach yelled at a fan and called him nigger at a University Basketball game. After the fan filed discrimination complaint, UH did not investigate or admonish the student coach for his discriminatory behavior. The student coach was the UH basketball coach Riley Wallace's son. A $30,000 fine was awarded to the fan. The student coach apologized after the decision and settled to pay an unspecified amount of damages. The University appealed the HCRC decision, arguing the student coach actions did not make the University liable and that he was exercising his First Amendment right to free speech. The Hawaii Supreme court decided in 2003 <u>State v. Hoshijo</u>, that the "N-word" is a fighting word, not protected by the First Amendment.[41]

CHAPTER VI
Speech by Judge JackTanner, Testimony by AALA, and Correspondence

Judge Jack Tanner, the first African American Federal Judge, appointed by President Jimmy Carter in the Western District, participated in the 1991 Hawaii Civil Rights Commission conference. He gave his speech to AALA and it is now printed for all of you to read. Judge Tanner died in 2008. The African American Museum in Seattle has a display on Judge Jack Tanner, who was an ardent advocate for civil rights.

SPEECH BY US.S. DISTRICT COURT JUDGE JACK E. TANNER, DECEMBER 10-11, 1991 AT THE ILIKAI HOTEL: "NATIONAL OVERVIEW AND EVALUTION OF CIVIL RIGHTS."

Of course, it all started with the introduction of slavery into the colonies that would become the United States. The Supreme Court said it best in 1856 when it decided <u>Dred Scott v. Sandford</u>:

In the opinion of the court, the legislation and histories of the times, and the language used in the Declaration of Independence, show, that neither the class of persons who had been imported as slaves, nor their descendants, whether they had become free or not, were then acknowledged as a part of the people, nor intended to be included in the general words used in that memorable instrument.

It is difficult at this day to realize the state of public opinion in relation to that unfortunate race, which prevailed in the civilized and enlightened portions of the world at the time of the Declaration of Independence, and when the Constitution of the United States was framed and adopted. But the public history of every European nation displays it in a manner too plain to be mistaken.

They had for more than a century before been regarded as beings of an inferior order, and altogether unfit to associate with the white race, either in social or political relations; and so far inferior, that they had no rights which the white man was bound to respect; and that the negro might justly and lawfully be reduced to slavery for his benefit. He was bought and sold, and treated as an ordinary article of merchandise and traffic, whenever a profit could be made by it. This opinion was at that time fixed and universal in the civilized portion of the white race. It was regarded as an axiom I n morals as well as in politics, which no one thought of disputing, or supposed to be open to dispute; and men in every grade and position in society daily and habitually acted upon it in their private pursuits, as well as in matters of public concern, without doubting for a moment the correctness of this opinion.

Then in 1896 came the case of Plessy v. Ferguson, whereby the Supreme Court of the United States set forth the infamous "Separate But Equal" doctrine. The white race deems itself to be the dominant race in this country. And so it is, in prestige, in achievements, in education, in wealth and in power. So, I doubt not, it will continue to be for all time, if it remains true to its great heritage and holds fast to the principles of constitutional liberty.

Responding to the majority opinion, Justice Harlan dissented. An excerpt from his dissent is as follows:

There is no caste here. Our Constitution is color-blind, and neither knows nor tolerates classes among citizens. In respect of civil rights, all citizens are equal before the law. The humblest is the peer of the most powerful. The law regards man as man, and takes no account of his surroundings or of his color when his civil rights as guaranteed by the supreme law of the land are involved. It is, therefore, to be regretted that this high tribunal, the final expositor of the fundamental law of the land, has reached the conclusion that it is competent for a State to regulate the enjoyment by citizens of their civil rights solely upon the basis of race.

In my opinion, the judgment this day rendered will, in time, prove to be quite as pernicious as the decision made by this tribunal in the Dred Scott case". How prophetic he was. For all intents and purposes, for those of us who are assembled here today, "Civil Rights" for African-Americans, Blacks, Coloreds, Negroes, etc., started on May 17, 1955 when the Supreme Court of the United States handed down the decision in Brown v. Board of Education. Before that historic date, there had been only slavery, black codes, Jim Crow laws, blatant acts of violence, lynching, murder, segregation and discrimination. All of which were intended and designed to continue the ravages and vestiges of slavery against those who were descendants of slaves, and also against those of African descent who had never been enslaved. It was a time of celebration and rejoicing by many Americans. The millennium had been reached. The promised land was right in front of us. All we had to do was reach out for acceptance as first-class citizens of our country and we too could then benefit from the abundant resources of America.

Coming ten years after the end of World War II, Brown v. Board of Education was unexpected. It should have been anticipated because President Harry Truman had given the signal in 1948 when he issued the Second Emancipation Proclamation; that is, when he issued his Executive Order in May of 1948 desegregating the Armed Forces of the United States. He had come to realize that at long last the time had *come* for America to recognize African-Americans as first-class citizens. The Armed Forces of the United States were the first of our revered institutions to take such action. Even then there was bitter and great protest, within the respective services, against the President's action. It was sometime in 1963 before the "Jim Crow" units were eliminated from all units of the Armed Forces.

Still today, racial discrimination in the Armed Services of the United States is alive and well. The vestiges of the old days, before 1948, can be found both as to service personnel and civilian personnel in the United States and overseas. The appointment of General Colin Powell as Chairman of the Joint Chief of Staff did not eliminate racial discrimination from the Armed Forces. The confirmation of Associate Justice Clarence Thomas as a member of the Supreme Court of the United States did not eliminate racial discrimination from the federal judiciary. I must say, in all fairness, that the appointments of General Powell and Judge Thomas to such high offices does give hope and promise for the future of those two great institutions of America. I was just about two weeks away from graduating from law school when Brown v. Board of Education literally stunned America. What did such a decision mean to America? Was "Separate But Equal" self-operating or was there more to be done, and by whom?

For those of us who celebrated that great victory of May 17,

1955, joy and exuberance was to be a transit euphoria. We were suddenly and rudely awakened to the realities of life. Racism had become a way of life in America. All of our democratic institutions had become "racialized." Not even dynamite could dislodge hatred, distrust and frustration from white America.

I am sure that there are different opinions and judgments as to the history of civil rights in the United States. "Separate But Equal" was the order of the day at the time.

African-Americans were being subjected to the same treatment they were received as slaves before the Emancipation Proclamation. No one really knew just what Brown meant to the struggle of African- Americans in their quest for justice and human dignity.

Unfortunately Brown v. Board of Education did not eliminate the concept of "Separate But Equal" from the everyday life of Americans. Massive programs of resistance appeared, primarily in the South at the time. Public officials and private individuals rushed to shore up the ramparts defending their way of life that involved the African-American descendants of the good old days of slavery and the doctrine of "Separate But Equal." States rights interposition and intervention became the battle cry of the South. Some of us believed that we should push ahead in the Supreme Court to find out just what exactly was meant by "with all deliberate speed", in the desegregation of schools. We also wanted to shift the meager resources that were available to the North and West. Little did we realize, at that time, what was going to happen next. African-Americans responded to the massive resistance by organizing sit-ins, pray-ins, wade-ins, bus boycotts and other acts of civil disobedience. The south responded with police brutality, police dogs, fire hoses, bombings, lynching, murder and imprisonment. The whole world watched as African- Americans, with their white supporters in many instances, fought back against their oppressors with the meager resources that they had. They placed their bodies, their lives and their property on the line in the struggle for civil rights and human dignity. In 1957, Governor Orval Faubus of Arkansas, refused to allow nine (9) Black children into Central High School. President

Eisenhower sent federal troops to Little Rock and Daisy Bates led the children into the school.

In 1955 Rosa Parks refused to move from her seat on a bus in Montgomery, Alabama. Her arrest brought a young Baptist minister to immortality in history. He was the Reverend Martin Luther King, Jr. In 1962, we witnessed the "Freedom Bus Riders" who traveled under conditions of great physical danger throughout the south, testing public accommodations. Governor George Wallace stood in the door at the University of Alabama barring Autherine Lucy from entering. He shouted segregation in the past, segregation now, and segregation forever. President Kennedy federalized the Alabama National Guard. The Commanding General of the Guard asked Governor Wallace to move aside. He did. After his near assassination, James Meridith was escorted into the University of Mississippi by federal officials, at the direction of President Lyndon Johnson. Many new leaders appeared to fight alongside Thurgood Marshall and Roy Wilkins of the NAACP. They were Whitney Young of the Urban League, Jim Farmer of C.O.R.E., Deacons for the Defense who were the forerunners of the Black Panthers, Stokely Carmichael of the Students Non-Violence Coordinating Committee, and perhaps one of the most dynamic of all the protesters of the time, Malcolm X, who was assassinated at the peak of his life and influence in the Civil Rights movement. Of course there were others who made their contribution to the struggle. In the early 1960,s, there was a dramatic change in attitude and goals by many young blacks and many of their white supporters. Many rushed to the South to protest, with their presence and bodies, the use of force, violence and murder to hold off the protesters. "We shall overcome" served as the battle cry of the protesters. The cry of "Black Power" challenged the previous cry of integration. The violence escalated, culminating in the explosion of "Watts" in Los Angeles. Cities were set on fire across America and people were killed in the streets.

In August of 1963, Reverend Martin Luther King, Jr. led the massive "March on Washington" where he electrified the world with his "I have a dream" speech. Dr. King was one of the most effective proponents of non-violence in the history of the world, and he paid for it with his life.

In quick succession, America suffered a rapid progression of assassinations never experienced before or since in this country. Medgar Evers, the courageous field representative of the NAACP in Mississippi, fell in Jackson, Mississippi in June of 1963. President John F. Kennedy fell in Dallas, Texas on November 22, 1963. Martin Luther King fell in Memphis, Tennessee in April of 1968. Senator Robert Kennedy, the brother of John F. Kennedy, fell in June of 1968. There were others whom were not as well known. I think that I should interject here, there was specifically one aspect of the civil right struggle that I was personally and directly involved in. On June 21, 1963, I received a telegram at my home in Tacoma, Washington. It read as follows:

"AT FOUR O'CLOCK ON FRIDAY, JUNE 21, I AM MEETING WITH A GROUP OF LEADERS OF THE BAR TO DISCUSS CERTAIN ASPECTS OF THE NATION'S CIVIL RIGHTS PROBLEM. THIS MATTER MERITS SERIOUS AND IMMEDIATE ATTENTION AND I WOULD BE PLEASED TO HAVE YOU ATTEND THE MEETING TO BE HELD IN THE EAST ROOM OF THE WHITE HOUSE. PLEASE ADVISE WHETHER YOU WILL BE ABLE TO ATTEND. JOHN F. KENNEDY"

I received another letter in June of 1964 which read as follows:

National Association for the Advancement of Colored People
June 20, 1964
(Senate Letter No. 15)
Jack E. Tanner, Esq.
President, NAACP State Conference
1022 South Monroe Street
Tacoma, Washington
Dear Jack:

In a jammed chamber of the U.S. Senate there came the solemn moment on Friday, June 19, when the eleven title Civil Rights Bill was approved by a vote of 73 to 27. At that moment success was apparent and, as usually happens, the band wagon was loaded with persons claiming credit for what had been done.

This letter is written to you following a conversation with a daily newspaperman. He admitted that they had agreed that their news reporting in the Senate would focus on the role of Senator Dirksen and, in effect, ignore any other forces that may have had an effect upon approval of the bill.

However, the facts of history cannot be changed. It is a fact that the passage of the Civil Rights Bill has come about because of the tremendous and consistent work that you and others have done to make it possible. It is true that there have been some magnificent contributions by Senate leaders in this fight, but it was also you and the people that you represent who used your resources to make it possible for us to get a successful vote. Therefore, I wish to thank you and to let you know that this is your time of triumph.

Ever sincerely,
Clarence Mitchell
Director Washington Bureau

Then Vietnam occupied the attention of everyone in the United States. The anti-Vietnam movement reached its most vigorous protest among college students and young people in the United States. Kent State became a rallying call for the Vietnam protesters. Then as the war escalated and the body bags began coming home, violence and riots broke out across the country in protest of the war. Martin Luther King, Jr. took the civil rights movement into the Vietnam War. It has never been the same. People in America no longer were concerned or cared about the civil rights of Blacks in America. President Lyndon Johnson declined to seek reelection. Richard Nixon was elected President in 1968, after the riots at the Democratic Convention in Chicago. "Benign Neglect" of civil rights became the order of the day under President Nixon, who became the only President of the United States forced to resign the presidency of the United States. He did so in August of 1973.

There was some resurgence of the civil rights movement while Jimmy Carter was President - 1976-1980. He appointed more minorities and women to Federal judgeships than all the presidents before and after him.

We are now in the last decade of the 20th Century rehashing and debating the same issues that we thought had been resolved in the 60's. Once again, public officials and politicians are politicking racial issues to arouse white resentment against African-Americans. Only now, there are other minorities who are also the targets of racial or cultural resentment. Racism has been made respectable again by those seeking public office, who directly appeal to whites by covertly and overtly arousing their racial and cultural biases and anxieties.

What lies ahead for those who are the victims of bias and discrimination because of their race and culture? There is no one easy answer because those feelings of bias and bigotry are not just going to disappear from daily life in America.

During the times of the debates over the issue of statehood for Alaska and Hawaii, I was personally aware of the most heated arguments, by the opponents of statehood, for both Alaska and

Hawaii. The opposition was very much aware of the diverse cultural and racial populations of Alaska, and especially of Hawaii. Alaska became the 49th state in January of 1959 and Hawaii became the 50th state in August 1959. With the exception of California, no state in the United States has a larger or more diverse racial and cultural population. In my opinion no other state has more discrimination and segregation than Hawaii, that is, if racial and cultural bias and bigotry can be quantified in any meaningful sense.

Although you are separated from 48 other states by the vast Pacific Ocean, that bias and racial distrust reached out to you over the Pacific when the Senate of the United States refused to make your highly respected Senator the Majority Leader of the United States Senate. There is no other reason or explanation for what they did, except, of course, who he is and where he comes from.

It has now been about 128 years since President Lincoln declared the Emancipation Proclamation. It has been about 27 years since Brown v. Board of Education. It has been approximately 27 years since the Civil Rights Act of 1964 was passed, and it has been about 25 years since the Voting Rights Act became law. Still, African-Americans are struggling to gain access to first-class citizenship. They are struggling to make the playing field level so that America can truly become a color-blind nation. But, racism, sexism, and religious bigotry are still pervasive and invidious and a daily part of our way of life in America.

Racism and hate crimes are on the increase across America, in the schools, on the job, in the streets, and in the churches. There have been significant and dramatic changes in the cast of players, especially during the past decade. Unlike the 1960's, when civil rights and affirmative action programs were initiated and supported by the Federal government under the leadership of Presidents Kennedy, Johnson and Carter, the 1970's and 80's led to benign neglect and outright blatant opposition to civil rights and affirmative action by Presidents Nixon, Reagan and Bush.

Of course, we must also realize that the number of victims of racial oppression have increased dramatically since Brown v. Board of Education. The victims now are all of those in America who, by accident of birth, are not white, English-speaking Protestants with a preferably mid-European background.

We are now living in a time of economic recession, growing unemployment, bank collapses, corruption, cynicism and racial and religious clashes, all of which history teaches us are the foundation and underpinnings for bigotry and fascism. The economic, political and social resources of America will be sorely tested in the coming years. Civil rights for minorities will not benefit from the present situation. In the struggle over dwindling resources, whites will have the power and control. Progress in civil rights seems to be made only when America is in a good economic situation, or at the time of popular wars.

It is my judgment that any meaningful progress in the coming years must be initiated by the President of the United States. It is the leaders, in America, who must draw out the best in people. It is intellectually and morally dishonest for leaders, and would-be leaders, to appeal directly or indirectly to the worst in people. The worst in people leads inevitably to fears, anxiety, distrust and racism and fascism.

Demographics show that, by the year 2000, the work-force will consist of about 75% minorities, and that, in some areas, minorities will make up the majority of the population. It will be a time of turmoil; a time of divisiveness over affirmative action and quotas; a time of references to welfare queens and Willie Horton's; a time of pitting one minority against another; a time of racial and religious code words meant to deceive and confuse people; and, a time in which America is suffering from a sick economy, bitter arguments over abortion, poverty, lack of medical care, homelessness, troubled schools and ignorance. America cannot survive as a free democratic nation if the problems of minorities are ignored. The fate of minorities in the immediate future will determine the destiny of America as a strong economic force and influential world power.

AFFIRMATIVE ACTION Overcoming past history calls for governmental action. There must be meaningful economic, political, educational and social programs that actually create equal opportunities in America. The private sector of America must also initiate such programs. Self-reliance sounds good, but history has taught us that minorities have survived in America, through self-reliance. History also shows us that self-reliance is not enough to bring about equal opportunity, but with a combination of government action and private programs, self-reliance will then take care of itself. Self-reliance is not the answer in the quest for food, shelter, medical care or quality education. Minorities did not create the uneven playing field. It is impossible for minorities to pull themselves up by their bootstraps if they have no boots. Affirmative Action is as natural to America as motherhood, Chevrolet, Ford, Chrysler, General Motors, apple pie, hot dogs, Bud, and the phrase, "God Is On Our Side." America is what it is today because of affirmative action.

For more than two centuries in every aspect of American life, there have been preferences in many forms that were applicable primarily to white males from mostly Western and middle-European countries. They spoke English, and were Protestants. The preferences are now called "affirmative action", and "quotas". The preferences were established at a time when slavery, anti-Semitism, and a separate but equal existence were a part of daily life in America. Some of the early preferences were established primarily for European immigrants to America and veterans of wars. Later the preferences created were the G.I.Bill of Rights; preferences for farmers, and for businesses under SBA; for FHA financing, Chrysler and the Tennessee Valley Authority; for contracts and jobs allocated by cities, counties, states and the federal government that were controlled by white male, ethnic-specific political machines. The list is not meant to be exhaustive of all of the preferences which have and still now exist, but it is indicative of the scope of preferences. The only difference today is the identities of the beneficiaries of preferences. Instead of primarily Europeans, they are the descendants of former slaves, and now, of course, other minorities. Those in opposition to affirmative action seem to argue that slavery never happened in America, and that even if it did those now seeking to benefit from affirmative action programs, as others have in the past, are not themselves the victims of slavery, subject to bondage and freed by the Civil War and the Emancipation Proclamation. In other words, they are not direct victims of slavery, and therefore, should not be the beneficiaries of fair play and justice. One could reasonably argue that the people who believe that, could very well be of the same mind-set as those who believe the holocaust never happened; that President Kennedy wasn't assassinated by Oswald; that Santa Anna didn't massacre the defenders of the Alamo; that Indians didn't destroy Custer at the Little Big Horn; that the Japanese Empire didn't bomb Pearl Harbor; that there was no Crucifixion of Christ; and, finally, that all of those Americans in the past really didn't need the preferences after all. The vestiges and ravages of slavery, American style, together with the doctrine of "Separate but Equal", affected all African-Americans and still does. There are no distinctions made amongst victims of slavery. It is only fair and just that any and all compensatory programs, reparations and affirmative action should apply to all those who are the descendants of those people who were brought here from Africa. They are as much the victims of slavery as the slaves themselves. Just as all such programs should apply to all Jews who are the descendants of those Jews who were the direct and specific victims of the holocaust in Nazi Germany. America responded to the Jews' cries from throughout the world for justice for all Jews. America responded by the greatest reparations and compensatory program in the modern history of the world. America gave the Jews Israel.

There appear to be two primary arguments against affirmative action by the government. They are both specious.

Both were conceived by the opponents of civil rights. The arguments are that affirmative action is wrong because it is demeaning to its intended beneficiaries. The opponents of affirmative action always raise the false cry of some mythical white man who allegedly loses a job to a less-qualified minority. Yet, such a mythical person has never been identified by anyone at anytime. I am one of those who believes that if you are the descendant of the victims of slavery, the holocaust and other atrocities imposed upon human beings, then there should be no distinctions made based upon class, caste or ethnic background when it comes to receiving the benefit of preferential programs. All should share and share alike. I am also one of those who believes that it is only fair play and justice that the beneficiaries in interest of the oppressors who are part of the body politic have the continuing and ongoing duty and responsibility to pay compensation or reparations. Such duties, obligations and responsibilities are non-delegable for any reason. Everyone must pay their fair share to meet the cost of affirmative action, just as everyone is a member of the same body politic." Judge Jack Tanner speech in 1991.

In addition to inviting speakers, co hosting civil rights conferences, AALA testified before the Hawaii legislature on certain bills such as the Dr.Martin Luther King, Jr., holiday and divestment of funds from apartheid South Africa, and commented on historical events about African Americans in Hawaii, such as the lack of appointment of an African American Judge, the request of an appointment of an African American Judge, racial cartoons and racial offensive statements. Here are some of the written testimonies.
TESTIMONY IN SUPPORT OF A STATE HOLIDAY HONORING DR. MARTIN LUTHER KING, JR.

The Afro-American Lawyer's Association strongly urge this Legislative Body to enact Martin Luther King Jr.'s birthday, the 3rd Monday in January, as a State Holiday: Dr. Martin Luther King's contribution to the world as well as Hawaii can never be overemphasized. Dr. King spearheaded the civil rights movement from which many "minorities" or American people of color benefited. Most Hawaiian residents are "minority" people.

It is important for Hawaii to recognize and celebrate the struggle for equal rights and justice for everyone, regardless of their race, creed, color, sex, and religious and political beliefs. Such a holiday sends an important message to everyone that arbitrary discrimination should be cast aside in favor of unified sister and brotherhood.

It is curious that this State of "Aloha" with multiethnic diversity should be opposed to having a holiday honoring Dr. King, especially since it was the first State to ratify the federal holiday celebrating Dr. King's birthday. By not enacting this state holiday, a statement of opposition is in fact made and felt. Such opposition can be construed to mean a disagreement with the principals of equal rights for which Dr. King fought and died for. In response to the argument that Hawaii has too many holidays already, such an argument overlooks the fact that Dr. Martin Luther King's birthday *is* a federal holiday where no mail *is* delivered, where federal banking institutions are closed, where a majority of mainland states enjoy the holiday and therefore do not conduct business, and where all federal offices are closed. Therefore, only a certain amount of business can be accomplished any way. Additionally, the surplus of State funds last year was approximately *400* million dollars. A State holiday would cost no more than 2% of this surplus amount. With the holiday, there would be increased revenue through shopping, night on the town, sales and travel to outer islands.

Celebrating the birthday of Dr. Martin Luther King will bring pride to Hawaii as a state. To do otherwise will cause increasing concern and negative attention from citizens all over the world.

If Hawaii wishes to live the true meaning of its title as the Aloha State, recognition of Dr. King's birthday is right in step with the aloha concept.

AALA TESTIMONY IN SUPPORT OF ESTABLISHING A PERMANENT DR. MARTIN LUTHER KING COMMISSION

American Lawyers Association (AALA) strongly supports this bill which establishes a permanent Dr. King Holiday Commission. The past two years experience with an interim Dr. King Holiday Commission shows that good planning by dedicated individuals bring about a much needed educational awareness of civil rights in Hawaii. This past year, through the efforts of the Interim

Commissioners, a great civil libertarian, Dr. James Farmer, was brought to Hawaii. Dr. Farmer gave a number of lectures on civil rights in Hawaii. The community response was overwhelming. The educational value of preserving the image and goals of Dr. King should not be underestimated. Justice and equality, for everyone is a message which can never be overstated, and this is the underlying policy which the Dr. King commission emphasizes. Without the Commission, we believe events commemorating this great African American leader will not be as well publicized and perceived. For example, before the Commission was established, the parade commemorating Dr. King was a small group of people. The parade has now grown with over 20 groups participating from all ethnic, religious and political backgrounds.

We urge your passage of this bill."

AALA also served as a watch dog for civil rights. AALA filed a complaint against the Hawaii Dpt. Of Education for race discrimination and harassment on behalf of African American school children. As a result of AALA's petition regarding race discrimination in the Hawaii State Department of Education, the Hawaii State Department of Education issued a letter of findings of discrimination under Title VI of the Civil Rights Act. The complaint was made when a high school coach referred to a high school football player as the "N-word." This is the written decision and settlement by Gary Jackson of the U.S. Department of Education Office of Civil Rights.

U.S. DEPARTMENT OF EDUCATION OFFICE FOR CIVIL
RIGHTS, REGION X Henry M. Jackson Federal Building
Mail Code 10·9010
915 Second Avenue, Room 3310 Seattle, Washington 98174·1099
July 28, 1992 (206) 553-1930
Ms. Daphne Barbee-Wooten Afro-American Lawyers Association
Re: Hawaii State Department of Education Case No. 10921017
Dear Ms. Barbee-Wooten:

This letter is to notify you that the Office for Civil Rights (OCR) has completed its investigation of the above-referenced complaint against the Hawaii State Department of Education (DOE). You alleged that DOE discriminated against African-American students on the basis of race. Specifically, you alleged that the head football coach at Kalaheo High School made racially derogatory remarks during the fall football season of the 1991-92 school year.

OCR conducted its investigation under the authority of Title VI of the Civil Rights Act of 1964 (Title VI). Title VI prohibits discrimination on the bases of race, color, and national origin in programs and activities which receive Federal financial assistance from the U.S. Department of Education. DOE is a recipient of Federal financial assistance from this Department. The issue investigated by

OCR was whether DOE discriminated against African-American students on the basis of race when a high school football coach made racially derogatory remarks during the 1991- 92 school year. See 34 CFR 100.3(b)(1)(ii).

OCR's investigation resulted in the following findings of fact and conclusion with respect to the issue investigated:

Findings of Fact

1. The head football coach at Kalaheo High School was also a physical education teacher and tutor/instructor in the After School Instructional Program (ASIP) at Kalaheo High School is an academic tutoring program that all football team players are required to attend, while participating on an athletic team.

2. DOE has no specific written policies prohibiting the use of racially derogatory remarks.

3. DOE has an established policy regarding sanctions for possible teacher and coach misconduct which states that teachers/ coaches may be suspended or discharged for proper cause.

4. During a high school football game on September 21, 1991, while the coach was giving instructions to his players, he used racially derogatory remarks, in referring to an African-American player from the opposing team.

5. Kalaheo High School officials became aware of the alleged use of racially derogatory remarks by the coach on or about September 25, 1991, and suspended him from his position as coach and tutor/instructor in ASIP on September 25, 1991.

6. DOE conducted an investigation on September 30 and October 1, 1991, of the alleged use of racially derogatory remarks by the coach while coaching.

7. On October 3, 1991, DOE terminated the coach from his position as head football coach because of his use of excessive profanity and racial slurs in performing his coaching duties. On October 3, 1991, DOE also terminated the coach from his position as tutor/instructor in ASIP. The coach continued teaching P.E. at Kalaheo High School.

8. During DOE's investigation of racially derogatory remarks

by the coach, they did not inquire as to whether the coach used racially derogatory remarks while teaching P.E. DOE's stated reason for not inquiring into racially derogatory remarks while teaching P.E. is that the allegations against the coach concerned his language while coaching.

9. On October 9, 1991, a Federal district court issued a 10-day temporary restraining order requiring DOE to reinstate the coach to his positions as coach and tutor/instructor in ASIP.

10. On October 24, 1991, a Federal district court issued an order requiring DOE to reinstate the coach to his positions as coach and tutor/instructor in ASIP until appropriate due process procedures were completed for his termination from his positions as head football coach and tutor/instructor in ASIP.

11. It is DOE's position that, during the time of the coach's reinstatement, the coach received special oral instructions from the athletic director to refrain from the use of racial remarks while coaching. It is the coach's position that, during the time of his reinstatement, he received no special instructions from the athletic director or any other DOE official, to refrain from the use of racial remarks while coaching.

12. At no time during the coach's reinstatement did the principal talk directly with the coach regarding racially derogatory language. The coach received no written instruction from DOE to refrain from the use of racially derogatory remarks while teaching P.E.

13. It is DOE's position that the athletic director monitored the coach's behavior at football practices and games during the time he was reinstated.

14. After the coach was reinstated as head football coach pursuant to court order, he remained in this position until the end of the football season in early November 1991. The coach remained in his position as tutor/instructor in ASIP until the first week in December 1991.

15. Between October 24, 1991, and December 10, 1991, DOE took steps to go through the due process procedures as ordered by the Federal district court.

16. In a letter dated December 10, 1991, DOE terminated the coach from his position as coach, effective December 20, 1991, for verbal abuse, excessive profanity, and racial slurs.

Analysis and Conclusion

Title VI and its implementing regulation at 34 CFR Part lOO.3(b)(1)(ii) states, in part, that a recipient may not, directly or through contractual or other arrangements, on grounds of race, color, or national origin, provide any service, financial aid, or other benefit to an individual which is different, or is provided in a different manner, from that provided to others under the program.

OCR found that the head football coach made racially derogatory remarks to DOE student athletes on September 21, 1991, during a high school football game. Because the use of the racially derogatory remarks by the coach constituted different treatment on the basis of race, OCR concludes that the racially derogatory remarks discriminated against DOE African-American student athletes on the basis of race, in violation of Title VI at 34 CFR 100.3(b)(l)(ii).

DOE entered into discussions with OCR regarding the areas of noncompliance identified above. As a result of these discussions, DOE has agreed to take voluntary corrective actions as set forth in the signed Settlement Agreement (Agreement). A copy of the fully executed Agreement is enclosed.

OCR concludes that DOE will be in compliance with 34 CFR 100.3(b)(1)(ii), with respect to the Title VI issue investigated in this case, upon full implementation of the actions and commitments contained in the Agreement. Therefore, based on DOE's commitment to implement the actions specified in the Agreement which OCR will monitor, we are closing the above-referenced case as of the date of this letter.

This determination of compliance with Title VI is contingent upon DOE's implementation of the commitments set forth in the Agreement. DOE's failure to honor these commitments may result in further action by OCR with respect to this case.

This Letter of Findings is not intended, nor should it be construed, to cover any other issues regarding compliance with Title VI that may exist and that are not discussed herein.

You may request a reconsideration of this determination. Your request must be submitted in writing to this office within 30 days of the date of the Letter of Findings.

You may request reconsideration of only those findings that are adverse to you. This office will not review findings that are not adverse to you. In your request for reconsideration:

1. specify which findings were based on incorrect information;

2. specify which relevant facts were not included in the findings; and

3. provide any evidence that will support the above.

Your request for reconsideration cannot merely express general disagreement with OCR's findings.

Under the Freedom of Information Act, it may be necessary to release this document and related correspondence and records upon request. If OCR receives such a request, we will seek to protect, to the extent provided by law, personal information that, if released, could constitute an unwarranted invasion of privacy.

If you have any questions regarding this letter, please contact me or Felix E. Sandoval, Director, Compliance Division, at (206) 553-1930.

Enclosure

Sincerely,

Gary D. Jackson
Regional
Region X

Civil Rights Director

SETTLEMENT AGREEMENT

The settlement agreement reached is as follows:

I. INTRODUCTION

A complaint having been filed against the Hawaii State Department of Education (HDOE) and an investigation having been conducted by the Office for Civil Rights (OCR), U.S. Department of Education, under the authority granted by Title VI of the Civil Rights Act of 1964 (Title VI), the investigation (Case No. 10921017) having been completed and compliance concerns having been identified, which will be set forth in a letter of findings to HDOE, the parties have agreed to resolve this matter as follows:

II. GENERAL PROVISIONS

A. The parties to this Settlement Agreement (Agreement) are HDOE and OCR.

B. This Agreement shall become effective when the authorized representatives for both parties have signed the Agreement.

C. It is understood that this Agreement does not constitute an admission by HDOE of any violation of Title VI or of any other law.

D. The parties agree that this Agreement resolves only those compliance concerns identified by OCR in the investigation of Case No. 10921017. Any other compliance matters shall be dealt with and resolved in accordance with the procedures and standards in the regulation applicable to such matters.

E. In consideration of HDOE's implementation of the provisions of this Agreement, OCR agrees not to initiate enforcement proceedings with respect to the compliance matters addressed in the referenced complaint investigation. It is agreed, however, that in the event HDOE violates any provision of this Agreement, OCR will take appropriate measures to effect compliance with Title VI with respect to these matters.

III. REMEDIAL PROVISIONS

A. By October 1, 1992, HDOE will develop and implement a written policy that it does not sanction, permit or tolerate verbal harassment or abuse of students based on race, color, or national origin within its programs and activities by HDOE employees. The policy will include a commitment to promptly respond to allegations or information that verbal harassment or abuse on the basis of race, color, or national origin has occurred in its programs or activities. Further, where such discriminatory conduct is found to have. occurred, appropriate corrective measures will be promptly taken to ensure its programs and activities are operated in a nondiscriminatory manner, including appropriate steps to ensure the discrimination does not recur. Corrective actions may include disciplining the individual who has committed the discriminatory action, the provision of awareness training, and apologies to victims where appropriate.

B. By October 31, 1992, HDOE will provide written notice to all HDOE employees of the policies developed under section IILA. of this Agreement, and will explain these policies to HDOE employees during staff meetings.

IV. REPORTING PROVISIONS

By December 1, 1992, HDOE will provide OCR with a copy of the written policies developed under section III. A. of this Agreement; a copy of the notice issued to employees under section III.B. of this Agreement; and a written report stating how HDOE employees were provided an explanation of the policies developed under section IILA. of this Agreement, in accordance with section III.B. of this Agreement.

As a result of this decision, the Hawaii Department of Education has created a Civil Rights Division designed to hear complaints and act on discrimination claims.

CHAPTER VII
Bylaws and Minutes of African American Lawyers Association of Hawaii

Here are AALA's By laws and some of the minutes from AALA's early meetings.

The first meeting was noticed by Attorney William Harrison as follows:

To African American Lawyers in Hawaii
RE: Establishment of the
Hawaii Afro-American Lawyer's Association (HAALA)
Dear Gentlepersons:

In the past there has been some discussion between interested attorneys in the establishment of a Hawaii Afro-American Lawyer's Association. Recently Daphne Barbee, Sandra Simms, Andre Wooten and I had a meeting to consider whether interest in HAALA was strong enough to contemplate formalizing an organization. All parties to the meeting decided that there was more than enough interest in the establishment of HAALA set up an agenda for further meetings to determine officers of the organization as well as establish a direction and organizational goals. To this end we have suggested that an initial meeting be set for January 21, 1988, between the hours of 12:00 p.m. and 1:15 p.m. at the above offices. It was the opinion of all present that a luncheon brown bag meeting would be the most convenient for all interested parties.

The agenda for the first meeting will be the establishment of organizational goals, election of officers, the discussion of issues of importance to all Afro-American Lawyers as well as the establishment of a foundation for scholarships for potential black law students enrolled in the pre-admissions program at William S. Richardson School of Law.

We look forward to seeing as many of you there as possible and if anyone knows of other interested persons please feel free to let them know of this initial meeting.

Please contact me at the above number if you have any questions concerning the contents of this letter.

Sincerely,
William A. Harrison

AALA began meeting to discuss various concerns and project in

1988. Here are some of the minutes:

MINUTES OF AALA MEETING FEBRUARY 23. 1988

PRESENT: Sandra Simms, William Harrison, Daphne Barbee-Wooten, Solomon Johnson, Travis Stephens, Allison Jacobs-Pendragon, Pamela Boyd, Judy Weightman

DISCUSSION

Funds for Needy Pre-Admission Law Students.

The amount of $700.00 was raised for a young Afro-American preadmission law student who was experiencing financial difficulty. Establishing along term revolving financial aid fund was discussed. A separate Foundation for this purpose is being considered as this. is an organization goal.

Election of Officers. We will be electing officers at the next meeting.

We elected the following temporary officers: Treasurer - Sandra Simms. Secretary - Daphne Barbee-Wooten.

Sandra Simms has opened a bank account on behalf of AALA. We have a post office box, located in Mililani

Martin Luther King Jr.Holiday. There are some problems with getting the legislature to pass a State Holiday honoring Dr.

King's birthday. Lobbying and other legislative pressure should be utilized. There will be a walk around the State Capitol on

March 2, 1988 from 9:30 to 11:20. Bring your own sign. Contact your senator and state representative to make sure your voice is heard.

Jessie Jackson Campaign. There is a need for volunteers to help with mailing and telephone calls. Contact the Jessie

Jackson for President Campaign Headquarters.

New Business. Allison Jacobs-Pendragon volunteered to serve on the bylaws committee.

Sending people to conferences such as Women and the Law, where a special conference is scheduled for Women of Color in the legal profession. Was suggested. Since this is a new organization, our goals and philosophy will be discussed at the next meeting. Committees will also be set up.

AALA MINUTES AND AGENDA
MINUTES OF AALA MEETING
APRIL 27, 1988

PRESENT: William Harrison, Daphne Barbee-Wooten, Sandra Simms Solomon Johnson, Allison Jacobs-Pendragon, Wanda Pate, Pam Boyd, George Parker

SPECIAL GUEST: Attorney Mililani Trask EXCUSED: Andre Wooten, Judy Weightman DISCUSSION

Attorney Mililani Trask gave AALA members an excellent synopsis of what was happening with Hawaiian Right to Sue Bill and issue. The present bill which passed in the State Legislature this year has problems in that it allows the Governor three years to come up with a plan and does not provide for public input regarding the plan. Basically, the Hawaiian people do not presently have the right to sue the State for breach of trust regarding Hawaiian Home Lands and other Hawaiian property. The Federal Government, which has been in collusion with the State, is supposed to be the entity which looks out for any breach of trust on behalf of Hawaiians. In practice, Hawaiians have been ripped off by both the State and Federal Government so there is a real need for an effective right to sue bill.

At our next meeting, we will have another distinguished guest speaker, Mrs. Betty Harris, who is running for the Senate against on the Democratic ticket. Mrs. Harris is the first Afro-American female to run for Senator in Oahu. Please be present to discuss desires, ideas, politics and goals with her.

Jerry Wilson, Esquire, has been in contact with the Hawaii State Bar Association regarding grants. We need to have ideas and plans to obtain some of the available grant monies. Before we apply for a grant, we need to have federal tax-exempt status of a nonprofit organization. This will be presented further at our next meeting.

Daphne Barbee-Wooten
Secretary

MINUTES OF AALA MEETING

May 25, 1988 PRESENT: William Harrison, Daphne Barbee-Wooten, Sandra Simms Allison Jacobs-Pendragon, Judy Weightman, Andre' Wooten Paula Harris-White, Joe Mottl, Pam Boyd, and Marianita Lopez EXCUSED: George Parker, Wanda Pate, Solomon Johnson DISCUSSION Guest Speaker: Mrs. Bettye Jo Harris. Mrs. Harris has announced her candidacy for the 9th Senatorial District, located in Kaneohe-Kailua. She is running on the Democratic ticket against the present incumbent. Mrs. Harris discussed her concerns and goals and was open to campaign suggestions from AALA members. She has lived in Kaneohe for 26 years and has been active in Red Cross, YWCA, League of Women Voters, PTA and presently works at the Immigration Community Service Center as the Director. Some of her issues and concerns are quality education, drug problems, and family support programs. She is anti-death penalty and pro-choice. Mrs. Harris has an upcoming fundraiser which will be located at the Empress Restaurant, Chinese Cultural Plaza, Thursday, June 23, 1988, 5:30 to 8:30 pm. Tickets are $25.00 for a 5 course meal.

National Bar Association- William Harrison mentioned that the NBA will allow associations to join as members for $300.00 fee. Submission of the organization's By Laws are necessary before joining. The By Laws Committee will meet and have the bylaws presented before the next meeting. By Laws are also necessary before obtaining tax exempt status and available grants.

A suggestion was made to meet quarterly at someone's house so we can get more accomplished. This will be discussed at the next meeting which is on Wednesday, June 29, 1988 at 707 Richards Suite 300, Honolulu, HI.

On June 7, 1988, Mrs. Coretta Scott King was in town to observe and participate in the signing of the Bill which makes Martin Luther King, Jr.s' birthday a State Holiday. A reception at City Hall was held after the Governor signed the Bill. AALA Vice-President, Sandra Simms, Secretary, Daphne Barbee-Wooten and Board of Governors Jerry I. Wilson, Andre' S. Wooten and Wanda Pate were present. Sandra presented Mrs. King with a lei from and on behalf of AALA.

AALA MINUTES AND AGENDA
MINUTES OF AALA MEETING
MARCH 30, 1988

PRESENT: William Harrison, Daphne Barbee-Wooten, Jerry Wilson, Solomon Johnson, Allison Jacobs-Pendragon, Wanda Pate, Judy Weightman, and Andre' Wooten
EXCUSED: Sandra Simms
DISCUSSION
Election of Officers. We elected the following officers: President-William Harrison Vice-President/Treasurer - Sandra Simms
Secretary- Daphne Barbee-Wooten
It was moved and seconded that we have a Board of Directors. The following members were elected to serve on the Board of Directors: Judy Weightman, Wanda Pate, Andre 'Wooten, Jerry Wilson, Allison Jacobs-Pendragon, and Solomon Johnson.
If there is anyone else interested in serving on the Board of Directors, please bring it to our attention at the next meeting.
President William Harrison suggested we contact United States Supreme Court Justice Thurgood Marshall to have him as an honorary member of the Board of Directors for AALA. This motion was seconded and carried unanimously. President Harrison will write to Justice Marshall and let us know the status.
Discussion was also held on whether we can affiliate with the National Bar Association as an organization. William Harrison will check into this matter.
Committees. We set up the following committees. Fundraising-Chairperson Jerry Wilson
William Harrison
Wanda Pate
By Laws - Chairperson Allison Jacobs-Pendragon Judy Wieghtman, Andre' Wooten
The Fundraising Committee will look into available grants, specifically the grant being offered by the Hawaii State Bar for

educating the public on law.

Suggestions for use of the grant included establishing a low cost legal clinic, making educational videotapes of different aspects of law and being a lawyer for children, videotape of history of Afro-American Lawyers in Hawaii and Nationally.

Philosophy and Motto. We have decided on the following motto: **"Advancement of Human Rights and Justice"**. Our goals and philosophy will become more detailed after the bylaws committee meets to discuss this mater.

Legislative Action. There was a hearing on the divestment of Hawaii investments in South Africa. The Joint Committee of Finance and Judicial Committee unanimously passed a bill supporting the divestment measure. AALA provided written testimony in support of this bill.

The bill establishing a state holiday in honor of Dr. Martin Luther King has been passed out of committees and is sure to pass the House this year.

Publicity. Jerry Wilson saw on Channel 5, a program endorsing South Africa as an excellent tourist spot. Jerry will write a letter to Channel 5 expressing our viewpoint about the program and the South African government.

A press release about our organization and newly elected officers will be prepared by Wanda Pate.

Judicial Appointments. We endorse Sandra Simms as a Judge. Letters should be sent to the Judicial Selection Committee on her behalf. Andre' Wooten brought up the fact that Judge Daniel Heeley will support AALA's endorsement of Sandra Simms. There may be other influential people who will help us in recommending an Afro-American judicial candidate.

Please bring up suggestions at the next meeting.

Jury Panels. Most State and Federal jury pools do not include persons of Afro-American ascent. A letter will be drafted requesting Federal Courts select jurors who are in the military so that a more fair representation of Afro-Americans will be in the jury pool. President Harrison will draft this letter.

Allison Jacobs-Pendragon will send a letter of condolence to Tommy's family, a nice family court clerk who recently died of a heart attack, on behalf of AALA.

AALA MINUTES AND AGENDA
MINUTES OF AALA MEETING
August 31, 1988

PRESENT: William Harrison, Daphne Barbee-Wooten, Allison Jacobs-Pendragon, Judy Weightman, Andre' Wooten, Yvonne Chotzen and Solomon Johnson

DISCUSSION:

BY LAWS: AALA reviewed and adopted By Laws for our organization. Copies of the By Laws will be available at our next meeting on September 28, 1988. With the By Laws, we can now request National Bar Association membership and apply for the many grants which are available locally and nationally.

FINANCIAL AID: Judy Weightman recommended AALA write to Doris Pascua of the University of Hawaii Law School to open a Pre-Admission Scholarship fund. President William Harrison will call or write to Ms. Pascua and make a report at the next meeting.

GRANT WORKSHOP: Allison Jacobs-Pendragon will be attending a grant proposal workshop September 12th through the 16th, 1988. AALA approved financial appropriation in the amount of $50.00 for partial payment of the enrollment fee in the grant workshop. Allison Jacobs-Pendragon will give us a report and share information at our next meeting.

GENERAL DISCUSSION: President Harrison received a phone call about Charles Marsland's Re-election ad which is running on t.v. There was a complaint that the ad was racist in its portrayal of Afro-Americans. After viewing the ad and with general discussion among members, AALA took no action as it was agreed that the people portrayed in Marsland's anti-drug ad were "an amorphous group of people" who looked "local or Puerto Rican" and the ad was not necessarily aimed at Afro-Americans.

A letter will be written regarding the Tony Williams case where an Afro-American was shackled in a courtroom and an extra security door placed at the entrance of the courtroom, creating the impression of guilty and dangerous before the evidence was presented to the jury. Letters will be sent to State and Federal Judges regarding the lack of Afro-American jurors in the jury pool.

AALA MINUTES AND AGENDA
MINUTES OF AALA MEETING
September 28, 1988
PRESENT: William Harrison, Daphne Barbee-Wooten, Allison Jacobs-Pendragon, Andre' Wooten, Sandra Simms
DISCUSSION:
Vice-President & Treasurer Sandra Simms gave a financial report. Attorney Jerry I. Wilson contributed a generous gift of $250.00 to our organization. Our budget has a balance of $437.00 as of the end of September. We have ten dues paying members. William Harrison will need some of this money to purchase our stationary which we will have by the next meeting.

Members approved a Motion to send a letter of appreciation and thanks to Attorney Wilson for his generous and thoughtful donation. Thank you Attorney Wilson.

A motion was made and passed sending Dr.John Edwards of the City Liquor Commission a letter commending him for doing an excellent job on the Commission. One of his many accomplishments includes the suspension of liquor license to Hyatt Regency due to race discrimination practices which occurred at Spat's Discotheque.

Allison Jacobs-Pendragon will travel to Connecticut to attend a grant project seminar. She will return with useful information on what grants are available and how to apply and obtain certain grants.

Sandra Simms has the spirit of aloha and suggested a quarterly meeting at her house. The meeting will be a get together party as well as a business meeting. The date will be announced at our next meeting.

AALA members voted to co-sponsor a Reproductive Freedom

seminar at the University of Hawaii with Hawaii Women Lawyers.

The suggestion of putting on a writing clinic for people who plan to take the Bar Exam was presented and approved.

A legal problem involving the Afro-American Associations Newspaper was presented to AALA. Mediation was discussed as the better route to solve the problem.

AALA MINUTES Meeting of
10-16-88

PRESENT: Yvonne Chotzen, Daphne Barbee-Wooten, Sandra Simms Andre Wooten

DISCUSSION: Sandra Simms received application forms for the Judicial Openings. The Judicial Selection Commission has a new waiver of confidentiality form. The waiver includes a candidates waiver of confidential information to medical and hospital records, and to credit reports. AALA feels the waiver is too broad and violates the Constitutional right to privacy. While some waivers are relevant to obtain a judicial appointment, such as disciplinary complaints, credit ratings have nothing to do with being a Judge nor do confidential medical records. AALA agreed to write a letter to the Judicial Selection Commission asking them to rewrite their waiver. In the waiver, there is no opportunity for the judicial candidate to respond or even know of any adverse information obtained.

Participation in the Dr. Martin Luther King holiday celebration was discussed. There will be a parade, bell ringing, and black tie ball on January 14, 1989. Tickets to the Ball are $35.00 per person, It will be held at the Ilikai Hotel Ballroom and includes speakers, food and entertainment. See Andre Wooten for tickets.

MINUTES OF AALA MEETING
December 28, 1988

PRESENT: William Harrison, Daphne Barbee-Wooten, Andre' Wooten

DISCUSSION:

Happy New Years to Everyone!

Thank you Sandra Simms and Family for the Christmas Party! These minutes will incorporate business discussed at the Christmas Party and our last meeting.

AALA will be offering assistance to anyone who wants to take the Hawaii State Bar Exam. Please contact Sandra Simms for more information.

AALA will be participating in the Dr. Martin Luther King Parade scheduled for January 16, 1989 (Now An Official State Holiday). Yvonne Chotzen and Solomon Johnson have volunteered to drive their Mercedes Convertibles which seats four. If you are planning to be in the parade, please be at Ft. DeRussy at 8:30 a.m. on January 16, 1989. Please contact Daphne Barbee-Wooten for more information. See you there. We have contracted with an artist Lillie James to prepare a banner which can be reused in future events. She is also preparing a logo.

There will be a formal ball sponsored by the Afro-American Association of Hawaii at the Ilikai Ball Room, January 14, 1989 honoring Dr. Martin Luther King Jr. Tickets at *$35.00* are still available.

We need to begin some fund-raising projects and get our tax exempt status so we may apply for grants.

The NBA has raised its rates from *$300.00* for associated members to $ *600.00*. In view of this rate change, the membership will be asked whether we should individually apply or proceed with association membership.

Flowers were sent to Judy Weightman who is recovering from surgery and to William Harrison who just recently became a father for the third time.

AALA AND AGENDA MINUTES MEETING
JANUARY 25, 1989
PRESENT:William Harrison, Daphne Barbee-Wooten, John James Allison Jacobs, Wanda Pate, Judy Weightman, Sandra Simms and Andre' Wooten
DISCUSSION :
The University of Hawaii Law School Foundation will be

happy to assist us in establishing a preadmission scholarship fund for minority students. President Harrison will write to the UH foundation to establish this scholarship. This scholarship can either be a rotating loan or a straight on grant. Attorney Andre' Wooten has contributed *$200.00* to UH foundation for the pre-admission scholarship fund. Grants. Attorney Allison Jacobs was unable to attend the grant program and she suggested that AALA send away for a "Directory of Financial Aid for Minorities". The membership approved the acquisition of this directory which will be useful for finding out types of grants and financial aids available. The costs of this directory is $42.50. Attorney Jacobs will refund the balance of the *$50.00* from the $42.50 to AALA. The directory will be made available to all AALA members and interested persons upon inquiry. Other additional information regarding grants is available at the grant room located at the Bank of Hawaii downtown branch.

At our next meeting we will be collecting dues for membership in AALA. Membership dues are *$20.00* for lawyers and *$15.00* for law students or other attorneys who are not members of the Hawaii State Bar.

Afro-American Association Newspaper. Attorney Andre' Wooten informed AALA that the Afro-American Association Newspaper is looking for contributing writers. Attorney Allison Jacobs volunteered to write a legal column for the Afro-American Association Newspaper for the month of April, 1989. Attorney William Harrison volunteered to write a legal column for the newspaper for the month of June, 1989. Anyone else who is interested in writing a legal column for the newspaper please feel free to volunteer and submit a legal column or a column on anything of interest to the public.

AALA discussed the various types of fundraising which we need in order to accomplish our goals such as establishing scholarships for needy students and other note worthy causes. One event in particular concern is the upcoming American Bar Association which will be held in Hawaii the month of August 1989. AALA is in the process of working out when and where we can have a meeting and gathering

place for ABA conventioneers. Attorney Simms will be following up
on this information. One excellent suggestion for a fundraiser was
presented by Attorney James. Attorney James is a music promoter
in addition to being a lawyer. Attorney James indicated he would
be willing to assist in putting on a musical concert as a fundraiser
project for AALA.

Anyone who has ideas as to which musician to bring to Hawaii as
a fundraiser please present these ideas at the next meeting. Attorney
Barbee-Wooten suggests Prince however, any other names will be
seriously considered. It should be noted that Prince would definitely
sell out the Blaisdell Arena if he came. We must have our non-profit
status prior to the musical concert. The MLK parade was a success.
It was very lively and well attended. AALA had two cars, thanks
to Attorney Yvonne Chotzen and Attorney Solomon Johnson. The
banner and the logo are finished and will be presented and shown
to the members at the next meeting. The video tape of AALA's
participation in the parade will also be available for viewing at the
next meeting.

In UH Law School, the preadmission program was created to
admit applicants who were not represented in the mainstream.

AALA MINUTES AND AGENDA
MINUTES OF AALA MEETING
MARCH 30, 1989

PRESENT: William Harrison, Daphne Barbee-Wooten,
Wanda Pate, Sandra Simms, Andre' Wooten

Jerry I. Wilson, Yvonne Chotzen, Solomon Johnson, Michael
Ragsdale

DISCUSSION

GUEST SPEAKER- Mr. Jeremy Harrison, Dean of the University
of Hawaii Law School

Dean Harrison presented the following statistics regarding Afro-
American applications for admission in the University of Hawaii
Law School.

In 1987, there were 394 applications for admission into UH Law
School's 75 positions. 15 of these applicants indicated they were

Afro American. One was a Hawaii Resident who was admitted into the Preadmission Program. One was a New York resident who was admitted into the Preadmission program but did not enroll. One was admitted to regular class but declined. Of the remaining 12, 5 applications were not completed and seven were not admitted. In 1988, there were 410 applications for 75 seats in the UH Law School. 9 were Afro-American. Out of these 9, 2 were Hawaii residents,, and 2 others had a Hawaii nexus. 6 applications were incomplete. One applicant was denied, One was admitted to the regular class, and one was admitted to the preadmission programs but did not enroll.

In 1989, there were 459 applications for 75 seats in UH Law School. 7 were Afro-Americans. Out of these 7, 6 were non residents with no nexus to Hawaii. 2 of these were admitted, and 1 application was incomplete. One applicant has a Hawaii nexus and was admitted. At this time it is unknown who will accept admissions and enroll.

These statistics are based upon applicants who indicate they are of Afro-American ascent. There may be some Afro-Americans who have listed themselves as other or mixed or another ethnic group they identify with. The UH Law School gives preference to those applicants which have a Hawaii nexus.

The trend nationwide is a decline of Afro-American enrollment into Law Schools.

AALA MINUTES AND AGENDA
MINUTES OF AALA MEETING July 26, 1989

PRESENT: William Harrison, Daphne Barbee-Wooten, Sandra Simms, Wanda Pate, Solomon Johnson, Yvonne Chotzen

DISCUSSION

AALA voted to have a separate non-profit organization , the AALA Foundation, which can be used to provide financial assistance and obtain grants for the benefit of Afro-Americans and other minorities in the Hawaii and Federal legal community.

Wanda Pate volunteered to assist an Afro-American who is imprisoned at Halawa Facility. He wrote to the organization for direction into legal matters and other information.

On August 6, 1989 the ABA Commission on Opportunities for Minorities in the Profession co-sponsored a breakfast program, "Breaking the Cycle: Promoting Minority Interests from within the Majority Bar" with AALA. The program was excellent and AALA members were able to network with a variety of inspiring, intelligent, thought-provoking Afro-American lawyers, judges, professors and supportive persons.

AALA MINUTES AND
AGENDA DISCUSSION

At our next meeting we will be discussing upcoming events for celebrating Dr. Martin Luther King's holiday. We have been requested to participate in the Martin Luther King Day Parade. Anyone who is interested, please attend the meeting. We still have the banner that we used for last years' parade. We need volunteers for automobiles and ideas for the parade.

At the last AALA meeting, Attorney William Harrison and Attorney Andre' S. Wooten discussed a proposal for a monetary award to high school students. It is agreed that AALA members would contribute money which would go toward an award for the best written article concerning the civil rights movement and Dr. Martin Luther King - its meaning and relevance in today's society. This award will be announced in the Afro-Hawaii newspaper and AALA will be listed as the sponsor. Attorney Wooten's letter and notice is enclosed.

AALA recently appeared in the Honolulu Star Bulletin as an organization in support of pro-choice.

Attendance at AALA meetings has not been good at the last couple of months. We need your help in order to make AALA a viable and important voice in the community at large. We get many calls from different organizations asking for our input. Judge Heely has written to us and we have made contact with the ABA Minorities in the Profession Organization, a powerful national group.

Elections for officers will take place soon. Please make your nominations in writing by January 1990. Please attend the next meeting.

A.A.L.A.
Afro-American Lawyers Association
MINUTES OF AALA MEETING
November 16, 1990

PRESENT: Sandra Simms, Daphne Barbee-Wooten, Andre Wooten, Judy Weightman, Andrew Mirikitani, Pam Boyd.

END OF YEAR REPORT

The Association marked the new 1990 year by participating in the Martin Luther King Jr. parade on Monday, January15, 1990.

AALA monitored and submitted testimony on a number of issues affecting the African-American community during the 1990 legislative session.

In May, AALA sponsored a booth at the Afro American Cultural Festival at McCoy Pavilion, distributing educational materials and addressing questions concerning the law and the legal profession.

Tutoring for the July bar examinees was provided free of charge by members.

On October 29, 1990, the Association submitted testimony on the proposed rules of the Civil Rights Commission which would have given the director of the commission the discretion to dismiss complaints without a hearing in certain circumstances, effectively denying complainants their right of due process. A copy of the testimony is available for inspection. Contact Pam Boyd, 548-6273. During the November election, AALA was represented at a rally held at Trinity Missionary Baptist Church in support of Senator Daniel Akaka.

AALA also joined other members of the legal community, including Hawaii Women Lawyers and the Filipino Lawyers Association urging voters to reject the constitutional amendment that would have increased from five to ten, the minimum number of years of practice required for district court judicial nominees.

NEW Nominees are being accepted for 1991 AALA officers.

BUSINESS Enclosed herewith are: (a) ballot, (b) form letter of transmittal, (c) ballot envelope, and (d) return envelope

After marking your ballot, place it in the envelope marked "Ballet Enclosed" and seal that envelope. Then sign the "Letter of Transmittal", printing or typing your name under the signature. Return your sealed ballot and the signed letter of transmittal in the envelope addressed to AALA. Ballots must be received before close of business on Wednesday, January 2, 1991. Candidates for the respective officer positions receiving the most votes shall be declared elected to their respective offices. Write-in candidates are encouraged.

Once again, the Association would like to be represented at the annual Martin Luther King, Jr. parade scheduled to be held on Monday, January 14, 1991. Members who are interested in participating, please leave your name and telephone numbers with Pam Boyd at 548-6273.

In conjunction with the parade festivities, the Third

Annual Dr. Martin Luther King, Jr. Banquet will be held on Friday, January 18, 1991, from 7:00 p.m. to 12:00 midnight, at the Hyatt Regency Waikiki. We would like to reserve a table for as many members and their guests who wish to attend. Please send your check in the amount of $35.00 per person to Pam Boyd, Office of the Public Defender, 1130 North Nimitz Highway, Suite A-135, Honolulu, Hawaii 96817, so that we may reserve a table a.s.a.p. Dress: Business suit, including military forma, semi-formal, and after-five.

The invited guest speaker is Major Fred A. Gorden, Commanding General, 25th Infantry Division (Light), Schofield Barracks, Hawaii. The ticket price includes complimentary admission to an after-party at Spats

Night Club. The president of the National Bar Association has expressed an interest in visiting Hawaii spring/early summer.

Persons interested in hosting our guest, please contact Bill Harrison.

We want to renew our efforts to sponsor an essay contest in conjunction with Black History Month. Three prizes will be awarded for the best essays: First prize will be $175; second, $50; and third, $25. Judges will be needed. Volunteers please call Pam Boyd In 1991 we want to renew our efforts to increase our visibility and participation in bar-related activities, and support and advocate programs of benefit to the African- American community. We need each other. Get involved.

Find your niche!

A.A.L.A.
Afro-American Lawyers Association
MINUTES OF AALA MEETING
February 9, 1991

PRESENT: Rustam Barbee, Sandra Simms, Sandra Donnell-Smith, Jerry Wilson, Daphne Barbee-Wooten, Andre' Wooten, Jeff Bates, Pam Boyd, Judy Weightman, Andy Mirikitani

OLD BUSINESS: Per diem judgeships applications are due by February 15, 1991. Sandra Simms reported that Jerry Wilson has written letters to Chief Justice Herman T. F. Lum, Gerard A. Jervis of the Judicial Selection Committee, and Mayor Frank F. Fasi regarding the lack of black judges in the State. Congressman Neil Abercrombie, State Senator Tony Chang and Senator Daniel Inouye have expressed their support for the appointment of a black judge. Simms also advised the members that her application is pending with the Judicial Selection Committee.

Daphne Barbee-Wooten will send a letter to the Hawaii Bar Association's Judicial Selection Committee regarding their refusal to accept Daphne's nomination of Ms. Donnis Thompson to the committee. Daphne was advised that a selection had been made prior to the nomination deadline.

A letter will be sent to Governor Waihee requesting his support for the appointment of a black judge to the state bench.

LEGISLATION: A bill to establish a permanent Martin Luther King Commission will be heard on February 12, 1991, at 1:30 p.m. The commission is presently a voluntary organization.

Daphne Barbee-Wooten is looking for volunteers to serve with her or possibly replace her position on the Civil Rights Commission. The commission meets twice a month. Her appointment expires in June, 1991. Jerry Wilson was recommended as a potential replacement appointment.

NATIONAL BAR ASSOCIATION: The NBA wants a Hawaii chapter. However, chapter dues are $300 regardless of the size of a given chapter. Simms will submit a letter to the NBA requesting an exception to this rule given the membership of AALA.

NEW BUSINESS: Pacific Business News has approached Barbee-Wooten regarding press for AALA. Barbee-Wooten will follow-up on our contact.

Andre' Wooten is looking for assistance in sponsoring a one-half day EEO seminar towards the end of 1991. If you have any ideas and/or want to participate, please call him. He's also looking for input regarding alternatives to incarceration program.

Judy Weightman attended a panel at the University of Hawaii focusing on sexist-racist speech. Anthony Lewis, columnist for the New York Times, was present. Interestingly enough, there were no Afro-Americans represented on the panel. This subject is a potential seminar topic. The law school wants to continue the discourse. Where do you stop racist speech and who decides?

ALOHA: Sandra Donnell-Smith, an October 1990 admitted to the Hawaii Bar, has relocated from Washington, D.C. Ms.Donnell-Smith is a 1983 graduate of the American University, Washington College of Law. Currently, she is teaching science, math, history, and English at the hearing-impaired program at Pearl City High School. She monitors and supervises a part-time teacher in the hearing- impaired .math and history classes; provides sign language interpreting services for student mainstreamed into hearing classes; and advises ninth grade hearing-impaired students.

MEMBERSHIP DUES: Dues are $20.00 annually and are due and payable to AALA. Rustam Barbee is our treasurer.

ESSAY CONTEST: Membership voted to extend the deadline for the Martin Luther King, Jr. essay contest to March 31, 1991.

T-SHIRTS: Wilson will investigate AALA tee shirts with logo.

AALA MINUTES
FOR MEETING OF 4-13-91

Present: Andre' S. Wooten, President, Rustam Barbee, Treasurer, Khaled Mujtabaa, Judy Weightman, Andy Mirikitani, Solomon Johnson, Daphne E. Barbee-Wooten, Annette

1. Treasurer's Report by Rustam A. Barbee, Treasurer $200.00 in bank account. There are eight dues paying members. Please send your dues ($20.00 per year) to the Treasurer for 1991.

2. Old Business

a   Civil Rights Essay contest: No one has written an essay. After discussion, it was decided to reopen the essay contest for 18 years or younger, Afro-American students, to write an essay on Civil Rights. Fliers will be passed out at the annual Afro- Festival at Kapiolani Park, June 22, 1991. 1st Prize $200.00, 2nd $75.00, and 3rd Prize $25.00. The prize will be awarded on September 1, 1991. Essays to be submitted by August 15, 1991. AALA members will judge the essays. If you know of a student who could use the money and has an interest, please give her/him a copy of the enclosed flier.

b.   Afro Festival: Aala members will be having an information booth at the Afro-Festival in Kapiolani Park, June 22 and 23, 1991. Please come and participate. Bring business cards and any other information for the general public. For more information, see enclosed flier.

c.   Donation to Links: $100.00 will be donated to the Links, Inc., for scholarship purposes.

d   Civil Rights Seminar: Aala will present a seminar in November, 1991 from a plaintiff's perspective. A letter of invitation to United States Justice Thurgood Marshall has been sent. All members should contact Andre' S. Wooten, 545-4165. Thoughts of what areas you would like to present, ideas on the best place to have the seminar are appreciated.

MINUTES OF MEETING OF
AFRO-AMERICAN LAWYERS ASSOCIATION
NOVEMBER 15, 1991

PRESENT: JOSEPH MOTTL, JUDGE SANDRA SIMMS, DAPHNE BARBEE, ANDRE WOOTEN, PAMELA BOYD, JUDY WEIGHTMAN, WANDA JONES, RUSTAM BARBEE, JERRY WILSON, SHARON MUJTABAA

OLD BUSINESS:

1. Sandra Simms will be sworn in as a District Court Judge of the Honolulu Division, First Circuit Court, on Monday, November 25, 1991, at 4:00 o'clock p.m. at the Hawaii State Supreme Court. Reception to follow.

2. Ms. Sharon McPhail, President of the NBA and retired Judge Tanner will be guests of AALA at a dinner set for December 12, 1991. Time and place to be announced later.

NEW BUSINESS:

1. Nominations for 1992 officers are due by Wednesday, December 11, 1991.

2. The membership voted over one dissenting vote to increase membership dues for 1992 from $20.00 to $25.00.

3. A committee was established to draft a policy regarding the representation of AALA before the news media. Committee members include Jerry Wilson, Andre Wooten, Daphne Barbee, and Pam Boyd.

4. Judy Weightman was appointed to investigate our federal tax status and state registration status.

5. AALA has been invited to attend meetings of the board of directors of the Hawaii State Bar Association as a nonvoting board member.

6. Judy Weightman expressed her concern about the recent October bar examination passage rate. The multi state section of the examination is causing problems for a number of women and minorities who take 'the examination. Judge Daniel Heely is chairman of the Bar Examination Committee. Unanimous vote to write a letter to Judge Heely expressing our concerns. Daphne

Barbee volunteered to draft the letter.

MINUTES OF MEETING OF AFRO-AMERICAN LAWYERS ASSOCIATION HELD ON JANUARY 19, 1992

PRESENT: JUDGE SANDRA SIMMS, DAPHNE BARBEE-WOOTEN, ANDRE WOOTEN, JEFFREY BATES, PAM BOYD, RUSTAM BARBEE, HANK SIMMS, WILLIAM HARRISON, JUDY WEIGHTMAN and ANDREW MIRIKITANI

1. Monday, January 21, 1992, MLK Jr. Parade.

2. Thank you letter from NBA President, Sharon McPhail, dated December 30, 1991, letter indicated that the National Association hopes to resolve the matter of our affiliate status and pulling us into the active work of the NBA. Individual applications for membership was encouraged (Note: Sharon McPhail was in February Ebony issue, a nice article).

3. Daphne presented a draft of her letter to Judge Heely regarding the lower percentage pass rate of the last Bar Exam in Hawaii. Letter was circulated, amendments made and letter approved.

4. Andre' presented a draft of a press statement regarding the University of Hawaii Athletic Director, Stan Sheriff, AALA, and Afro-American Association to present the conclusion of the inquiry and report on the status of the Afro-American athletes at the University of Hawaii.

The report addressed the three areas in a series of six recommendations:

1. Emotional and career counseling.
2. Medical treatment.
3. Student discipline.

AALA and Afro-American Association leaders are pleased to announce the creation of an expanded counseling program for Afro-American athletes at U.H. This will be personal counseling with an emphasis on academic support.

5. January 1992 edition of Afro-Hawaii News printed AALA Award winning civil rights essay by a 17 year old, Senior of Punahou High School, Sarah Bremer.

Nomination:
Daphne Barbee-Wooten, Andre' S. Wooten, Jerry Wilson

1. Goals and Suggestions: Seminar within the Criminal Justice System - Fall - Minorities in the criminal justice in Hawaii - we are 6% of the prison population compared to 3% general population based on recent census.
Essay contest again.
Register with university to become a registered organization of the university - want to establish a big brother/sister organization. When students arrive in August - have a reception in August or September or, a picnic.
Listing with Chamber of Commerce.

2. Encourage those of you job hunting, to consider submitting your applications to the Department of Attorney General.

3. Daphne filed a Complaint on behalf of AALA regarding coach Smith of Kalaheo High School making racist remarks about black players. Filed with U.S. Civil Rights Commission, Department of Education.

4. Write to State agencies who contract private firms for legal work to ensure that minority law firms are being considered.

5. Letter to AG's, Governor and Corporation Counsel to be drafted encouraging hiring of minority lawyers.

6. Contact Bar Foundation to get application for project this year. Perhaps the Criminal Justice System project will possibly include a job fair or, speakers bureau to involve students. Draft a letter to include the AG's Criminal Justice Division.

7. Rotate place of meetings from each members house. The next meeting in March will be held at:

Presentation of plaque with newspaper announcement from Star Bulletin awarded to Judge Simms on her appointment as HNL District Court Judge.

AALA BYLAWS
NAME AND AFFILIATION
ARTICLE 1

Name. The name of this association shall be the Afro-American Lawyers Association, hereinafter referred to as AALA.

Affiliation. AALA shall be an affiliate of the National Bar Association, Inc.

ARTICLE II
PURPOSE AND SCOPE

Purpose. The purpose of the AALA is to promote the advancement of human rights and justice.

Nonpartisanship. The purpose of AALA shall be pursued without regard to political partisanship.

Scope of action. AALA shall take all legitimate action in furtherance of its purpose, including legal action, action on legislation, action with respect to governmental administrative agencies, and educational and informational activities.

ARTICLE III
MEMBERSHIP

Qualifications. All persons who have graduated from law school and are living in the State of Hawaii may be members of AALA. All persons who are in law school and are living in the State of Hawaii may be associate members of AALA. Honorary membership may be conferred upon persons selected by the Board of Governors.

Termination. Any person may terminate his/her membership in AALA by written notice to the secretary.

ARTICLE IV
MEETINGS

Annual Meetings. There shall be an annual meeting of the membership once in each calendar year at a time and place determined by the Board of Governors. A meeting notice shall be *mailed* to each member not later than two weeks prior to each annual meeting. The business of the annual meeting shall include reports of AALA activities and such other matters as the Board of Governors may deem proper.

<u>Special Meetings</u>. Special meetings of the membership may be called at any time by the Board of Governors and shall be called by the Board of Governors upon the written request of ten percent of the membership. A meeting notice shall be mailed to each member not later than five days prior to each special meeting.

<u>Quorum</u>. Ten percent of the membership shall constitute a quorum at any membership meeting.

Section 4. All membership meetings shall be open to the public, but voting shall be only by members.

Section 5. <u>Rules</u>. <u>Roberts Rules of Order</u> shall govern meeting procedures to the extent not inconsistent with these By-Laws.

ARTICLE V: BOARD OF GOVERNORS

Section 1. <u>Duties</u>. The direction, business and affairs of the AALA shall be the duty and responsibility of the Board of Governors.

Section 2.1 <u>Members terms</u>. The Board of Governors shall consist of not fewer than five, nor more than fifteen Governors, as the Board of Governors shall determine. All Governors shall be members of AALA. The Governors shall be elected by the membership. A vacancy on the Board of Governors may be filled by appointment by the remaining Governors, and the Governor so appointed shall serve out his/her predecessor's unexpired term.

Section 2.2 <u>The nominees</u>. The nominees for the Board of Governors who receive the greatest number of votes (up to the number of vacancies to be filled), shall be elected to the Board and shall serve for a term of three years, commencing on the first day of January following their election and ending on the first day of January three years later.

Section 2.3 A Board member may resign in writing to the Secretary at any *time*. The Board of Governors may remove a Governor from office for repeated failure to attend five regular Board meetings.

Section 3 <u>Meetings Quorum</u>. The Board of Governors shall hold monthly meetings on the last Wednesday of each month unless it decides otherwise. Special meetings may be called by the President or any three Governors. Reasonable notice of regular and special shall be given to all Governors. A quorum for the conduct of business by the Board of Governors shall consist of three Governors. Meetings of the Board of Governors shall be open to the membership, but voting shall be only by the Governors.

Section 4. Committees. The Board of Governors shall establish such standing and special committees as may be necessary for the purpose of AALA

ARTICLE VI
ELECTIONS: BOARD OF GOVERNORS

Section 1 <u>Annual Election</u>: . The Board of Governors shall designate a date for the annual election of Governors each year during the month of December.

Section 2 <u>Public Attendance Nominations</u>. The Board of Governors shall appoint a nominating committee which shall consist of not fewer than three members. At least two months before an annual election, the nominating committee shall mail a notice of its proposed nominees for Governors to each member. Any member may submit additional nominations to the Nominating committee not later than one month before the annual election; provided any nomination so submitted shall be accompanied by a statement signed by such nominee that he/she is willing to serve as a Governor if elected.

Section 3 <u>Ballots</u>. The Secretary shall prepare and mail ballots which shall contain the names of all candidates for Governors. The ballots shall not distinguish between candidates nominated by the nominating committee and candidates nominated by submission from members. A ballot shall be mailed or delivered to every member at least two weeks before the annual election.

Section 4 Nominating committee not later than one month <u>Voting</u>. Members shall vote by mailing or delivering their ballots to the address designated thereon. No ballot shall be counted unless it is received at the designated address on or before the date of the annual election. Ballots need not be signed, but the signature and address of each member voting shall be placed on the envelope containing the ballot. Ballots shall be opened in a manner to preserve the secrecy of the ballot.

ARTICLE VII OFFICERS

Section 1.1 Officers. The officers of AALA shall consist of a President, Vice President, Secretary, and a Treasurer.

Section 1.2 The duties of the officers shall be as follows:

Section 1.3 The President shall preside at all meetings of the Board of Governors. He/she shall appoint all necessary committees.

Section 1.4 The Vice President shall perform all duties of the President in his/her absence.

Section 1.5 The Secretary shall record and prepare the minutes of each meeting to be presented to the Board for correction and approval.

Section 1.6 The Treasurer shall be responsible for all funds of the organization, and shall present a quarterly written financial report at the regularly scheduled Board meeting unless requested to provide an additional report.

Section 2. Election: term. The officers shall be elected by the Board of Governors from among its own members at the first meeting of the Board following the annual election of the Governors. Each officer shall serve until his/her successor is elected. The Board shall fill any office which becomes vacant from among its own members.

ARTICLE VIII
AMENDMENTS

The Board of Governors shall mail proposed amendments to these By-Laws to the membership at least two weeks before they are to be voted upon. An amendment may be proposed by action of the Board of Governors or by a written submission to the Board of Governors made by any member. The vote on a proposed amendment may be by mail ballot to all members or by vote at the annual membership meeting. An amendment shall be adopted upon approval by two-thirds of the votes cast on the question; provided ten percent of the membership cast a vote on the question.

ARTICLE IX

ADOPTION OF BY-LAWS AND FIRST ELECTION

These By-Laws shall be adopted by a two-thirds vote of approval of the charter members of AALA who Live in Hawaii and are present at the organization meeting on August 31, 1988. The charter members of the organization duly elected to be officers and Board members shall serve according to the adopted provisions of the By-Laws for one year or until the next annual meeting.

CHAPTER VIII
Awards, Travel, Significant Achievements, Further Readings and Updates to 2020

In January 2009, the Friends of Civil Rights selected the African American Lawyers Association for a civil rights and justice award. They received an award along with President Barack Obama's sister, Maya Soetoro-Ng at a reception that was held at the Pacific Club. AALA received Senate and House resolutions and award from Mayor Hanneman and Congressman Abercrombie, for their work on civil rights.

At the Civil Rights Award Ceremony, January 2009, Danielle Conway, Daphne Barbee-Wooten, Andre Wooten, Rustam Barbee, Sandra Simms.

While there are no African American judges in Hawaii in 2009, African American lawyers are getting more respect and publicity because President Barack Obama, an African American lawyer, was raised in Honolulu. There is an increase in tour and interests by African Americans to visit Hawaii and see the roots of President Obama. President Obama and his wife, attorney, and partner Michelle Obama, visited Hawaii at least two times a year and met with some of the African American Lawyers Association members, Sandra Simms, Daphne Barbee-Wooten, and André S. Wooten in 2004 before he ran for Presidential election.

**First Lady Michelle Obama, Judge Sandra Simms and Daphne
Barbee-Wooten in Honolulu.**

Several members of the African American Lawyers Association
traveled with the National Bar Association for international trips.
The National Bar Association is an international legal organization
formed by African American Lawyers and Judges who were not
admitted to the American Bar Association due to segregation pre
1959. It has become an organization for civil rights and working
for minority lawyers and judges. Attorney General Eric Holder is
a member. In 2009 and 2010, AALA members hosted the NBA
Judicial meeting in Honolulu. A reception was held at Bishop
Museum, attended by over 100 African American Judges from all
over the United States.

**President Shana Peete, husband Johnny Vevre, Judge Beverly Hayes-Sipes
(Detroit, MI), Judge Denise Langford-Morris (Circuit Court, Pontiac, MI),
Daphne Barbee-Wooten, Bernice Krause, Jamilla Jarmon, Andre Wooten,
Loan Shillinger. Seated to the right: Mark Valencia, Sandra Simms.**

Attorneys Andre and Daphne Barbee-Wooten traveled to Botswana, South African, and Zimbabwe with the National Bar Association in 2004. Judge Sandra Simms and her husband Hank Simms traveled with the National Bar Association to Ethiopia in 2006. In 2008, Daphne Barbee-Wooten Andre Wooten, Sandra Simms, Karen McKinnie, and Judge Marie Milks and Mr. William Milks traveled to Cuba with the National Bar Association. Educational discussions about the legal systems in the various countries and what we can do to assist them in their legal process was the travel theme. Travelling taught us about other countries legal and social concerns and how we could improve our legal system. In Botswana Daphne Barbee-Wooten met with Justice Unity Dow, who is a Supreme Court Justice in Botswana. The discussion amongst Botswana attorneys was adoption for children whose parents have AIDS. AIDS is the highest killer and 1 out of 4 children have become orphans as a result. Child support enforcement was discusses. Another discussion was the stealing of herbal plants indigenous to Africa by major pharmaceutical companies, who then patent the plants in the United States and try to sell it at highly inflated prices worldwide. There have been successful lawsuits against these patents by the Botswana government and the attorneys. It is also theft of culture such as art and song. The famous song in the Lion King, "In the Mighty Jungle the Lion Sleeps Tonight" was originally a song sung by a South African man. The song was recorded and brought back to Hollywood and thereafter copyrighted in an American's name without giving credit to the South African. The song became a hit in the 1960s and 1970s and then again when the Lion King was performed on Broadway. The descendants of the creator of the song in South Africa sued and won a portion of the proceeds.

A travelogue was published in Mahogany Newspaper in 2004. Mahogany is a black owned newspaper published the Afro Hawaii News and Mahogany once a month in Hawaii. Owner Ron Williams has lived in Hawaii and published since the 1980's. He also published the Hawaii Black Business and Professional Directory on an annual basis.

Here is a portion of the travelogue which I wrote about the trip to Africa.

TRAVELOGUE 2004

We live with the hope that as she battles to remake herself South Africa will be like a microcosm of the new world that is striving to be born. Nelson Mandela.

South Africa: Johannesburg.

Amandla.

We left Hawaii for New York, then to South Africa on an airplane. The flight takes 16 hours from New York then a stopover in Senegal. Finally we arrive in South Africa. Husband is cranky, having to sit in cramped quarters for so long. I am cranky with jet lag, it is exactly 12 hours ahead Hawaii time. Our group of National Bar Association (NBA), an organization of Black lawyers and judges from the United States, meets with the tour guides for Global Exchange, and are bused to the Hotel.

I'm struck by one thing, it's cold! In June. Summer. 12hours ahead and 20 degrees colder than home. It's also modern a big city. The freeways are 4 lanes- one lane more than Honolulu.

We arrived at the Hotel, which is posh, posh, in Sandton. The elevators have televisions in them. This is a different Africa than what is shown on American television. Our tour guides, Global Exchange, a politically socially aware tour group from San Francisco, gets our bags and room keys ready. It is 12:00 a.m. We are to meet and greet South African lawyers and Judges at 4:00 p.m. I'm beat. When we get to our swank, swank room, I sink into the oversized bed and collapse until 3:30 p.m. Then I get ready for the meet and greet reception.

In the grand ballroom, there were 50 or so very distinguished looking people. I introduced myself to a nice looking couple. The man had just been appointed a Judge. The woman was his former law partner. Her name is Lindelani Sikhitha. They told me the most lucrative law to practice in South Africa is property law. I told them I did some criminal law. They told me there is no money in criminal law in South Africa. I told them some lawyers in the U.S. can make a lot of money in criminal law, defending people like Michael Jackson. I said I would give up my other clients just to represent Michael Jackson. The Judge responded by saying he would give up his judgeship to represent Michael Jackson. I wish the best for Michael Jackson, I believe he is innocent, but he could have hired me. I am not the only lawyer or Judge who would not mind representing him. The food at the reception is great, lots of different fruits, vegetables, chicken and meat. My husband is a meat eater. He ate every meat there was, kudu, buffalo, wildebeest, impala, gazelle, wart hog crocodiles, goat, lion, elephant, zebra and giraffe. He lost 10 pounds, just by eating meat at every meal. Neither he nor I got sick. I'm a vegetarian, but did not go hungry. After eating, mingling, some speeches were made. Claps were given. Hands were shook. Business cards exchanged. Then jet lag got the best of me and I made my way back up the elevator to the room and the oversized bed with many pillows.

The hotel overlooked the city which was huge and sprawling. It could've been New York. I felt like a country hick.

The second day began with a tour of Soweto. Soweto is a city built on the outskirts of Johannesburg. During apartheid segregation, Africans lived in Soweto, and worked for whites in Johannesburg. Soweto is where many freedom fighters lived, Nelson Mandela, and Bishop Tutu, Oliver Tambo just to name a few. Soweto is poor. We met activists who were continuing to fight against oppression. The government installed prepaid water meters in Soweto. If you don't prepay your water, you are without. This has incensed residents who cannot afford water, which should be free. A group of activists go out daily and disengage the prep paid water meters.

The government has also installed prepaid electricity machines in Soweto. Poor people cannot get electricity unless they prepay. Bands of people go out and hook up free electricity as soon as government officials leave the area. We met with the activists, courtesy of Global Exchange, bought t-shirts and gave donations for the cause.

We ate at Wandies for lunch. It is a famous restaurant where many activists ate and met during the resistance to apartheid. Wandi opened his restaurant during apartheid, when it was illegal for Africans to be in business. It now is a thriving restaurant where business cards of famous people are placed on the wall. We added our business cards. The food is good. After a filling lunch, we visited the Regina Mundi Church. The church had a Black Madonna stain glass window, paints of the struggle and leaders and African drums. Upstairs there was a photo display of the struggle against apartheid. We also stopped at the corner where Hector Pieterson was shot by police. Hector Pieterson was a teenager who was involved in the student movement against learning Afrikaans instead of his own native language. There is a memorial brick wall where he was killed and a museum honoring the youth of Sharpesville. After Hector and others were killed in 1976, there was massive uprising by the students at schools in Soweto. Several hundred of young children were shot by police on June 16, 1976. Now June 16th is a holiday known as Youth day in remembrance of the young persons killed in the struggle. It was a somber and pivotal moment in South Africa's history with the youth leading the challenge. There was a mass funeral at the Regina Mundi Church for the youth.

In Soweto, people were very nice. Children dressed in school clothes smiled and waved hello. Women with large bundles on their heads walked without missing a beat. On a couple of street corners, goats were slaughtered with a machete for weddings and funerals. Some of the houses had walls of cement or rock around them. Others had burglar bars on the doors and windows. The houses were of varied bright colors, hot pink, green, blue, brown, patchwork. In the distance were two towers- nuclear power plants in Soweto that served Johannesburg during apartheid. They are painted with multi colors in an African pattern.

Back at the hotel, we caught up with the news on the elevator television, and I dropped off in a jet lag coma in the room. When I woke up, it was time for a visit with the U.S. embassy in Johannesburg. My husband had disappeared. I went to the U.S.

Embassy with others in our group. I meet with various lawyers, and politicians. The U.S. Embassy reception was held on the patio of a house in Johannesburg and was COLD. Most of us huddled near the outside oven. There were a couple of obligatory speeches, pats on the back and handshaking. My husband returned to explain he got lost in the mall attached to the hotel which is larger than Ala Moana Shopping Center. It took him a couple of hours to find his way back to the hotel. A large statue of Nelson Mandela is located in the Mall, surrounded by shoppers and jewelry stores.

At the Sandton shopping mall, as I looked for presents, a store keeper asked me if I knew Peebo Bryson. She said Peebo Bryson was her favorite singer. She played his music in the store. She sang his songs in between showing me fancy African dresses. When I left, she asked me to tell Peebo Bryson he has a fan in South Africa. Peebo, if you read this, you are informed.

We began the next day with a seminar comparing the South African sentencing laws and prison system with U.S. sentencing laws and prison system at the Mandela Foundation. The Mandela Foundation building serves the community for events and seminars. It was rumored that Nelson Mandela himself would be at the seminar. Unfortunately the closest we got to seeing Nelson Mandela was driving by his house and taking photos of a statue at the Mandela Foundation.

The Honorable Bridgitt Sylvia Mabandla, Minister of Justice & Constitutional Development - Government of South Africa since April 2004, the Honorable Penuell M. Maduna, former Minister of Justice of South Africa, Judge Arthur Burnett Sr. (Senior Judge of the Superior Court of the District of Columbia, November, 1998) Cheslan America, Director of the Bureau of Justice Assistance, a joint project of the South African Ministry of Justice and Constitutional Development and the Vera Institute of Justice spoke. Cheslan previously served under the Inspecting Judge of Prisons. As the National Chief Inspector of Prisons he was responsible for monitoring the treatment of prisoners and prison conditions. In 1997-1998, Cheslan worked for the investigative unit of the South

African Truth and Reconciliation Commission where he researched
and documented human rights violations during the apartheid era
and acted as a liaison with community groups. Law Professor Kevin
Malunga from South Africa, and NBA President, Clyde Bailey Sr.
moderated the discussions. Justice Albie Sachs of the Constitutional
Court of South Africa gave a brief overview of the justice system in
South Africa.

At the seminar, Judge Burnett emphasized the need to do away
with the three strikes bill which authorizes imprisonment for life
upon a third conviction in the United States. The U.S. Prisons are
overflowing. There are over 2 million prisoners in the U.S., the
largest prison population in the world. The privatization of prisons
has turned incarcerating people into big business and profits. Many
inmates work for less than 25 cents per hour making popular clothing
apparel and other products such as furniture and computer systems-
the cheapest labor around and profitable for private industry.
Prisoners have become modern slaves in America.

One difference between the South African penal system and the
United States system is that in South Africa, prisoners retain the
right to vote. This makes the prison system more accountable and the
prisoners do not become forgotten people. In South Africa, torture
is forbidden and illegal. In the Unites States, torture is permitted
and encouraged despite the Eight Amendment prohibiting Cruel
and Unusual punishment. United States President Bush appointed
Alberto Gonzales as Attorney General to the United States, and
Gonzales approved legal memos narrowing the definition of torture
to only death or injuring an organ. In South Africa, the death penalty
is not permitted. In the United States, the death penalty is permitted
and executed, especially in Texas where Gonzales and President
Bush are from. Leaving the seminar I reflected on how different
these countries were and concluded that the present South African
government has learned from its wretched past and moved to a
better society.

We next visited the Constitutional Court of South Africa.
The Constitutional Court is located on a steep hill in the middle of

Johannesburg. It is the site of the Old Fort Prison Complex Number
4. Many people were brutally punished, tortured and murdered
at Number Four Prison. Mahatma Gandhi and Nelson Mandela
were imprisoned at Number Four. Parts of the prison walls of
Number Four have been kept intact and made into a museum
where tourists can visit and see firsthand the infamous prison.
One of the cells has documents written by Nelson Mandela and
when you press a button, you will hear one of his famous speeches.
It is the cell which housed Nelson Mandela when he was kept in
solitary confinement. Other cell blocks are open for viewing and
remind people of the past brutality. We ate lunch on the prison
grounds and met with Justices of the Constitutional court. Other
cell blocks are open for tours and viewing - a reminder of past
brutality. We had lunch in the exercise yard of the prison. Some
Justices of the Constitutional Court came to greet us. One Justice,
Albie Sachs, became tour guide and escort. Justice Albie Sachs was
a civil rights attorney during the apartheid era. His life was
constantly in jeopardy for his activity. He left the country in exile for
England and Mozambique. While in exile in Mozambique, in 1988
he was the victim of a car bombing which blew his right arm off.
He became a Justice of the Constitutional Court in 1994.

The Constitutional Court is a new building right next to
Number Four and was built there to remind us of our past as we
move onto the future said Justice Sachs. In contrast to the old musty
prison remains, the Constitutional court building is modern, and
vibrant. There are window on the ceiling, letting natural light shine
throughout the building. Huge wooden doors mark the entrance with
carvings from various African tribes. The red brick stairs leading to
the wooden doors are bricks from prison wall.

We stepped on parts of the old prison to get to the doors of justice.
The halls of the Constitutional Court are filled with colorful artwork
- not paintings of old dead white men. There are paintings from
Ethiopia, paintings by South African artists depicting the horrors of
the apartheid reign, paintings and sculptures from all over the world.
Justice Albie Sachs knew as much about the art work, the artists and

its meaning for being in the Constitutional court as he did about the legal cases and issues the court decides.

Justice Sachs pointed to a lone blue dress hanging on the wall on hanger near the entrance. He said it symbolized a dress found on an African woman whose body was recovered after the Truth and Reconciliation hearings. At the Truth and reconciliation hearings, a former police officer told about killing a young African woman who refused to name people in the African Nation Congress. She was shot and buried in a shallow grave. For years, no one knew where she was or what happened to her. When the shallow grave was uncovered, a blue dress covered her bones. The symbolic blue dress hanging in the Constitutional Court is a reminder of the destruction of the apartheid system and that unknown persons died for the struggle against injustice.

Daphne Barbee-Wooten in the South African Supreme Court

The court room is large and wide. The Justices chairs are in a semi circle so that they can see each other while they consider cases brought before them. The Court's facade is adorned with cow hide. Cows are sustenance in African diet, providing nourishment, and clothing for human beings. It is held in a place of prominence to remind Justices that like the cow, they too must nourish human beings with their decisions. Sunlight from the open windows skylight permeated the room.

The law library is several stories high, containing books from all over the world and computers of course. Justice Sachs showed us his court room chambers- which in addition to mountains of papers, contained artwork.

There are eleven Justices on the Constitutional Court which was established in 1994. In 2005, nine Justices were men, Chief Justice Arthur Chaskalson, Justice Pius Langa, Justice LWH Ackermann, Justice Tole Madala, Justice Dikgang Mosenenke, Justice S Ngcobo and Justice ZM Yacoob. Two were women, Justice Yvonne Mokgoro and Justice Kate O'Regan. Justice ZM Yacoob is blind. Chief Justice Chaskalson defended Nelson Mandela in 1967 sedition trial.

The Constitution Court has issued several important decisions since its inception in 1994. One of its first cases, State v. T. Makwanyane and M. Mehumu (June 1995), ruled that the death penalty was unconstitutional. Chief Justice Chaskalson wrote in the opinion:

The rights to life and dignity are the most important of all human rights, and the source of all other personal rights ... By committing ourselves to a society founded on the recognition of human rights we are required to value these rights above all others...This is not achieved by objectifying murders and putting them to death to serve as an example to others in the expectation that they might possibly be deterred thereby.

As we left the Constitutional Court and walked down the red brick steps that were once prison walls, a feeling of renewal and conscious growth surrounded me. South Africa has made great strides towards an egalitarian society. In the words of Nelson Mandela, To be free is not merely to cast off one's chains, but to live in a way that respects and enhances the lives of others.

The next day we visited the Kingdom of Bafokeng. As we exited the bus, youthful dancers and singers greeted us in loin cloth. They clapped, sang and danced as we walked between them soul train style up to the gate of the Queen Mother's House. The Queen Mother lived in a large 10 room brick home, with air conditioning, and a large yard, where tables had been placed for our luncheon.

In the center of the yard was a large sculpture of an alligator in a water fountain. It is the totem of Bafokeng. The alligator had two human legs, and symbolized the endurance of Bafokeng people. It is on their seals, flags and coat of arms.

Bafokeng, means people of the dew. The area where the Bafokeng people live and originate from is in northern South Africa and Botswana. During colonial racism era it was illegal for Africans to own land in South Africa. The Bafokeng people bought land from white farmers using Lutheran missionaries as front. They picked out the lands they wanted based upon oral history and knowledge of mining activities. When it became legal for them to own their land, title passed to the Bafokeng people and then surprise, surprise, platinum was found in the land. The Bafokeng receive 22% royalties for mining platinum and leasing it to mining companies. With the royalties, the Bafokeng people built a world class soccer field, shopping malls, and schools, sent youth to University and financed several small businesses.

The Bafokeng King, Kgois Leruo Molotlegi is a young architect and airline pilot. His older brother studied at Howard University and met the wife of the NBA president Clyde Bailey, Dr. Jean Bailey is a University Professor at Howard in Education department. Through Dr. Bailey's contacts, we were invited to have lunch with the Queen Mother and met with the King, and kikgosana (head persons) and the royal dancers, and royal musician, relatives and friends.

King Leruo spoke at the luncheon. Before he spoke, his paternal uncle chanted accolades griot style about the genealogy of the Kgosi and Bafokeng. At the end of his chant, people ululated and clapped in respect. The King had a royal umbrella holder whose job was to hold the umbrella over the king as he spoke. King talked about the progress of Bafokeng, and the politics and government and issues facing the Bafokeng people.

The Queen Mother also spoke and greeted her guests with a warm smile. She told a story about a blind man and a legless man being ostracized and placed in a forest. The two fought with each other until they figured out that if they joined forces, they could escape the forest. So the legless man rode on the head of the blind man, and steered them both from the forest. The morale, together with different strengths we become stronger and can be successful. She was a great and powerful speaker.

I brought kukui nut leis from Hawaii to give to the Queen Mother and the King.

My husband and I presented the kukui nut lei to the Queen Mother with a kiss on her cheek in Hawaiian style. I tried to present the other kukui nut lei to Kgosi Lerou but a woman dressed in black (chieftess of protocol) stopped me, saying I could not approach the King unless he agreed. She asked him, and he agreed we could approach him. I then gave him the lei, saying it was from Hawaii and he wanted to know where the flowers were. We told him flowers wouldn't have lasted the trip from Hawaii and that the kukui nut leis were a sign of virility and power, favored by the alii (Hawaiian royalty). He was very gracious and wore his lei during a photo opportunity with us. We subsequently turned this photo into a Kwanzaa card.

As we ate lunch the royal musicians of Bafokeng played music. The band had various instruments including a ram's horn, which is blown much like a conk shell in Hawaii. Gourds of various sizes make a xylophone, drums, and other percussion instruments. On the dancers and musicians legs were plant seeds twined around the ankle. As feet stomped in time, more music filled the air. One man chanted an African rap song, with resulting ululation from the women. He wore a leopard loin cloth around his torso and a lion covered helmet on his head. Throughout the luncheon, dancers performed a welcome greeting, a enjoy your lunch greeting, and a get to know you greeting. The dancers were stepping, stomping and jumping. Clapping and singing created an irresistible acapella rhythm. Some people from our group got up to join them.

After eating, meeting, greeting, clapping, dancing, blowing the kudu (rams) horn, looking and buying Bafokeng wares, we returned to the bus. Then to a brief stop at an open air market with bargains on various artistic sculptures, tables, cloths, baskets, chairs, carved from various wood. Everyone was exhausted upon return to the hotel. The next day, we traveled to Botswana.

We arrived in Gabarone, the capitol city in Botswana. The hotel was modern, with faxes and computers and email. It was set up for the business person. Nearly everyone in our group went to the computer room to check with our offices and to email friends and family.

Botswana has more trees than South Africa. On the day we arrived, which was my birthday, there was a reception at the national art gallery. The curator of the museum met us in the Gallery. There were paintings by the San people on display. The San people used dots in their paintings, resembling the aboriginal art of Australia. The curator told us that the San art work was renowned worldwide and used on magazine covers, often without the artists permission.

There is a thriving trademark and copyright law practice in Botswana. Pfizer sent some scouts to follow the San people around. The San are hunters and by eating a certain root, they were able to go for weeks without food. The Pfizer scouts found out what root the San people used and then brought it back to the United States, patented it as a diet pill. Botswana lawyers sued and won a victory against Pfizer. Now Pfizer is required to name the root, state it originates from Botswana and must pay a royalty on its sale.

After admiring San artwork, we were ushered to the courtyard where greetings, food and dancers awaited us. It was dark. There was a chill in the air. Shawls and jackets were worn. There was a large fire built in the middle of the courtyard. The food was displayed in black kettles. I bypassed the mapane worms, which someone said tasted liked shelled shrimp. As we ate, the dancers performed around the fire.

The next day we attended a seminar. The seminar compared American law with Botswana law. We were given an update on current Botswana law issues. The people were very friendly.

Justice Unity Dow was one of the speakers. Unity Dow is a famous Botswana attorney who sued the Botswana Supreme Court alleging sex discrimination in citizenship laws and won. See The Attorney General for the Republic of Botswana v. Unity Dow, 1992 BLR 119. She opened the door for women in Botswana. As a result of her law suit, women must be treated equally with men in Botswana and are guaranteed this right under the Botswana Constitution. She presented a paper about human rights in Botswana, portions of which proclaim:

Only when women are equal actors in the process can there be a legitimate claim that Africa is on the road to democracy. Justice Unity Dow.

After Unity Dow's case made international headlines, Botswana ratified the International Convention the Right of the Child, Convention on the Elimination of all forms of discrimination against Women, adopted a Policy on Woman, and established a National Council on Woman.

In 2000, Unity Dow was appointed to the High Court of Botswana as a Judge. She notes, "I have joined the growing number of women in Africa who are participating in redefining concepts of human rights, democracy, and good governance from inside."

She was very approachable and gave me a copy of her presentation, complete with autograph. Later, in a Botswana bookstore I was pleased to see three novels which Unity Dow wrote. I bought one, The Screaming of the Innocent which is a murder mystery set in Botswana. It was a quick and fantastic read and offered insight into some archaic cultural and political problems in Botswana. Other books written by her include Far and Beyond and Struggling Truths, written about life in Botswana. They present issues such as AIDS, sex abuse, corporal punishment in schools, colonialism and cultural perspectives on Botswana life.

Unity Dow is quite an accomplished person, civil rights activist, attorney, Judge, mother of three children and creative talented author. On top of all this, she looks like she is only 30 years old, petite, smooth silky chocolate brown skin, braids African style, and a huge welcoming smile. She is quite a dynamo.

We met many other knowledgeable attorneys and judges at the seminar, who shared their legal perspectives on Botswana and were interested in American legal system, especially family law issues such as child support enforcement, divorce property agreements, alimony, paternity and civil rights for all.

That afternoon, we were driven by bus to Ramatwase. Ramatwase is a village outside of Gabarone. Mma Ramatwase, who is the No. 1 Ladies Detective in Alexander McCall Smith's novels, hails from this town. In Ramatwase, we were greeted by the Chief, who is a woman. Her name is Kgosi Mosadi Seboko and she is one of only three women chiefs in Botswana. Chief titles are ordinarily passed to the oldest son in the royal family. In Ramatwase's situation, Chief Seboko's father was a Chief. His oldest son, her brother was not doing a good job. So she asked the council of elders and her uncles and aunts to be appointed chief. She laid out her plans and aspirations for the village. The council of elders met and voted to make her chief. She has done quite a lot for the village and is popular. She and her advisors met with us to discuss governance and their village. We sat in a circle under a grass hut. The chief was at the head of the circle. Elderly men advisors were to her right. Elderly women advisers were to her left. Children and guests (us) were seated in the middle. She talked about AIDS- a horrible problem in Botswana and in Africa. In Botswana, 40%of people have Aids. She called upon a teenager to talk about the abstinence program. He talked about spreading the word about AIDs and how it is acquired through sex. She introduced her liaison with the President of Botswana, a woman, who says they are consulted by the President on important issues. After the meeting, she offered us Bush tea. We sat around and talked with people. One elderly man wanted his photo taken, and informed me he was born in 1919. Chief Seboko explained that in legal matters, a Botswana citizen can choice tribal law and be tried by the Chief and her advisors instead of opting for legal process under the statutory system. The President of Botswana, the legislature and High Courts all consult with the Chiefs on matters of custom and culture.

The next day, we met with the President of Botswana. His name is Festus Magoe.

He welcomed our group to Botswana and talked about some of the political problems in Botswana. Foremost was AIDS. Botswana has the highest rate of AIDS in the world in 2004 at 40%. There were orphans who needed care after their parents died. He was upset that the U.S. Government would not provide funding for medicines which are very expensive. Instead, the U.S. would only grant monetary support for abstinence programs. He talked about the great stride Botswana was making in providing equal rights to woman. He pointed out that he appointed several women to his cabinet and will continue to increase the number of women in the judiciary.

He talked about his time in the U.S. attending Howard University law school and his work with the Congressional Black Caucus. He was extremely charming and articulate. Botswana has a democracy and he ran for election twice, winning both times. He is serving his last term. His Vice President is the son of the former President. He offered us tea and a photo opp with us.

Then he drove away to another meeting in his midnight blue Bentley, waving goodbye.

We next traveled to Chobe National Park for a meeting with wild life. There we met with wildebeest who made their presence known right from our porch, monkeys, who threw leaves at us from the trees, elephants who trumpeted as they made their way to the watering hole, gazelle flashing by, giraffes hovering over trees, hippos reveling in the water and the most exquisite colored birds, green yellow spotted red aqua, who lived in holes along the river bank. We took a boat ride on the Zambezi River. From the river, we saw the banks of Namibia, Mozambique, Zambia, Zimbabwe and Botswana. Along the river banks lurked crocodile who were fortunately too full to make a move on us. The hippos were very active in play and barely made way for our boats. Monkey and baboons walked freely near the river bank. Elephants came down in tribes to drink the water at dusk. There were eagles sitting atop the trees peering down, ready for fishing. The lions were hiding in the bush and did not feel like making a tourist appearance. We knew they were there because the morning newspaper headlines, featured the following story: LION DEVOURS A GUIDE AT NXABEGA LODGE

This was under the photograph of NBA president Clyde Baily and President Magae, receiving an award from the NBA.

At the banks of the Zambezi river, I placed ashes of my late father, Lloyd A. Barbee, and my uncle, Quinten Barbee. My father was a civil rights attorney in Wisconsin. My uncle was a journalist and federal employee in Washington D.C. They died within three months of each other the year before. Their ashes are now a part of Africa with lions, hippos, and elephants as their guardians.

After a too quick meeting with nature at Chobe, we went by bus to Zimbabwe, Victoria Falls. The African name for Victoria Falls is the Water that thunders. It is one of the world's natural wonders and the largest falls on earth. This is where Explorer Stanley met Dr. Livingston who was in Zimbabwe and made his famous remark Dr. Livingston I presume? There are rainbows among the numerous scenic routes along the falls.

That evening we were treated to an event with Zimbabwe dancers and musicians. The dancers electrified everyone with athletic graceful moves which tore up the house and put the roof on fire. The men wore feathers on their head and the women wore black and with grass skirts. The drumming was exceptional. Their drums were as tall as the drummers themselves. Musicians sang The Lion sleeps tonight in acapella. The song The Lion sleeps tonight is used in the famous play, The Lion King. The song was originally created in Africa by a South African man. His song was heard and then copied by a British songwriter who then copyrighted it as his own original work. Fortunately, with African lawyers at the helm, a law suite returned the copyright back to the original African creator and monetary royalties must now be distributed to his family.

The last day we stayed in Zimbabwe was another wonderful encounter with nature. The hotel was near a watering hole. At dusk, the animals put aside their disputes with each other and shared water at the watering hole in peace. Perhaps when humankind realize that the air we all breath, the land we all live on are watering holes we must all drink from, war and fighting will cease, like the animals at dusk.

(Note: This article was first published in Mahogany Newspaper, Honolulu, September-December 2004)

**Photo of King of Bafokeng with Attorneys Andre Wooten
& Daphne Barbee-Wooten**

**NBA Group Photo with Botswana President in Botswana 2004
President Magoe (in front and center).**

Justice Albee Sachs at South African Supreme Court

**Judge Mary Thomas (Illinois) and
Daphne Barbee-Wooten inside Bishop Museum**

Group photo with Attorney Julius Chambers

**Daphne Barbee-Wooten, Ramisha Knight, Judge Burns,
Sandra Simms and Elizabeth Fujiwara.**

Sandra Simms, Andre Wooten, Daphne Barbee-Wooten, Rustam Barbee
At civil rights award 2009.

AFRICAN AMERICAN LAWYERS
ASSOCIATION (AALA) UPDATES

It has been 10 years since the first edition of African American Attorneys in Hawaii was published. There have been several requests for an updated version so here it is..

There has been a decrease in African American attorneys practicing in Hawaii and in participation as members of the African American Lawyers Association. Some of the attorneys have moved to the mainland where job opportunities are greater and income is also better. Discrimination in Hawaii still exists based on race.

Attorney Rustam A. Barbee represented Honolulu Police Chief Louis Kealoha in a conspiracy trial that his wife's uncle stole their mail box. The jury convicted him in this high profile case. An appeal is pending. He served on Office of Disciplinary Council Commission. He was given a Resolution in 2009 for his outstanding work with the Disciplinary Counsel Commission Rustam A. Barbee enjoys a robust legal practice and caseload, focused on traffic and criminal defense. He golfs during some of his spare time.

Attorney Rustam A. Barbee came to Hawaii from Wisconsin, where he earned his J.D. in Madison. He spent 5 years as an Assistant Attorney General for the State of Wisconsin, then moved to Honolulu, to become an Assistant Federal Public Defender for 8 years. He then entered private practice of law. H likes "helping people with important legal matters in life". He dislikes legal stress such as rules and inflexible deadlines as being too rigid. He enjoys practicing law in Hawaii because it is more ethnically diverse that in the Midwest. Hawaii has a medium sized legal community so that a lot of fellow attorneys know each other and have interposal relationships. He wanted to call his own shots and make his own decisions about cases which he can accomplish being a solo practitioner, owning his own firm. He sat on the Hawaii Judicial Counsel, was CJA panel representative for the National Criminal Justice Act, Board member and past president of AALA, and sat on the Magistrate Selection Commission and Selection Commission for the Bankruptcy Judge. In addition, he lectured at Chaminade University and Honolulu Community College in Criminal

Justice, Evidence, Constitutional law, and Criminal Procedure.

Attorney Andre S. Wooten attorney is one of the original AALA members. He likes being an attorney as an independent business person, being his own boss, and helping people out of a difficult situations, such as being injured, wrongfully assaulted or unjustly prosecuted by the government. He moved to Hawaii from Seattle, due to the weather. He says a lawyer can litigate anywhere but only in Hawaii can you go surfing afterwards and forget about it. Hawaii living is a healthier lifestyle that on the Mainland. There is a need for African Americans attorney because a lot of African Americans are in the military and their families wind up going through the Hawaii state judicial system.

Hawaii has no history of slavery and was a place where slaves escaped to, like Anthony Allen, who was an African American whaler who jumped ship to live and remain in Hawaii as a businessman. Anthony Allen established a successful Inn in Waikiki. Because of the lack of a violent history, Hawaii makes living better although there is discrimination . The Police are not as intent on violence against African Americans as on the mainland.

His advice to new African Americans in Hawaii is "be diligent, get to know the community and you can be successful".

Atty. Wooten obtained significant monetary settlement for his clients. He graduated from the University of Washington-Seattle law school. His passion is videography and he presented Black History films about the African Kings and Monuments In Rome in 2019 at the Honolulu Art Museum Doris Duke Theater. He lectures and writes about Black History and does a public access television show called Color and the Constitution.

Here is an article he wrote for Mahogany about Color and the Constitution.

THE COLOR CODED U.S. CONSTITUTION HAS NEVER BEEN COLOR BLIND

Those who argue that the U.S. Constitution is "color blind" present totally false statements of facts.

The original U.S. Constitution enacted right after the Revolutionary War in 1779 was color blind. However, it was replaced by a Pro Slavery Constitution in 1789, which legalized and protected slavery in 7 specific places:

U.S. Constitution: Article. I. Section 2:

Representatives and direct Taxes shall be apportioned among the several States ..., according to their respective Numbers, which shall be determined by adding to the whole Number of free Persons, including those bound to Service for a Term of Years, and excluding Indians not axed, three fifths of all other Persons

Section 9:

The Migration or Importation of such Persons as any of the States now existing shall think proper to admit, shall not be prohibited by the Congress prior to the Year one thousand eight hundred and eight, but a Tax or duty may be imposed on such Importation, not exceeding ten dollars for each Person.

Article IV. Section 2.

No Person held to Service or Labour in one State, under the Laws thereof, escaping into another, shall, in Consequence of any Law or Regulation therein, be discharged from such Service or Labour, but shall be delivered up on Claim of the Party to whom such Service or Labour may be due.

Clause 1. Importation of Slaves ,General Purpose of Section 9 :

This section of the Constitution is devoted to restraints upon the power of Congress and of the National Government to respect affects the States in the regulation of their domestic affairs.

The above clauses sanctioned the importation of slaves by the States for twenty years after the adoption of the Constitution, when considered with the section requiring escaped slaves to be returned to their masters, Art. IV, Sec. 1, cl. 3, was held by Supreme Court Chief Justice Taney in <u>Scott v. Sandford</u> to show conclusively that such persons and their descendants were not embraced within the term ''citizen'' as used in the Constitution. This ruling shows clearly that historically the U.S. Constitution has never been color blind.

Separate planks bared Native American Indians from citizenship, and Asians and other non-whites were also barred from citizenship for over 200 years.

In 1857 the Dred Scott Supreme Court case, declared in Black and White type that a "Black man did not have legal rights which a white man was bound to respect." This decision lead to John Brown's raid on Harper's Ferry and the U.S. Civil War.

Despite the Civil War and the 13th, 14th and 15th Amendments of 1863, which state they were written to give the Freed Black U.S. citizens "the same rights as those enjoyed by the White citizens," Color based discrimination was re-codified into law nationally in 1896, by the U.S. Supreme Court in the Plessey v. Ferguson decision. In Plessy v. Ferguson, the Supreme Court ruled that "separate but equal" for Black and White was legal, an endorsement for segregation and racial apartheid system in America.

This color coded rights apportionment program, put in place in violation of the 13th, 14th and 15th Amendments, was only legally corrected with the Brown vs. Board of Education decision barring segregated public education in 1954 finally ruling that "separate is not equal".

So, for only 65 years of the total of 224 years of U.S. History, after the Revolutionary war ended in 1779, have American black citizens been legally considered equal in the eyes of the law. Given the 164 years of color conscious and color coded legalized discrimination practiced in the U.S.A., (Excluding the previous 250 year Colonial period discriminations) the only effective remedy for color discrimination is a color conscious remedy. The call for a color blind remedy, is simply a coded call for No Remedy for 224 years of discrimination."

In 2014 the NAACP awarded Daphne E. Barbee Wooten and Andre S. Wooten attorneys with the Distinguish Service Award. The awards were presented at the annual Martin Luther King dinner.

Attorney Daphne E. Barbee Wooten graduated from the University of Washington-Seattle law school. She worked as a Hawaii State Public Defender, then in private practice, then Sr. Trial attorney for the EEOC, then back to private practice, specializing in Civil rights. She was awarded the Women Making History Civil Rights Attorney of the

Year Award from Sisters Empowering Hawaii ~ Hawaii's Foremost Women's Empowering Organization in 2016.

Attorney Elizabeth Fujiwara, AALA member, graduated from the University of Hawaii law School. She was the former ACLU director. She is in private practice, In 2018, she filed a lawsuit against Hawaiian Airlines. Her client, African American had a noose displayed. Hawaiian Airlines argued that this was not a hostile work environment. The lawsuit settled for an undisclosed amount. Ms. Fujiwara writes:

"If you are not descendent of Norwegians, President Donald Trump, whom I consider a racist and white nationalist, does not want you in the United States. I learned on a trip back to my hometown, New Orleans, just a couple of years ago, that we are 1/432nd Black. My maternal side is of French descent – and one of our European cousins urged our cousin in New Orleans to do an extensive ancestor search. She learned that our great-great-great grandmother was a free slave. When she told me this, I started laughing! Why? Because so many in my family are racists. My cousin also learned that we were 1/28th Jewish. We are clearly all one.

What's with the percentages? It's an old Deep South tradition and now becoming a Washington one: one drop of Black blood and you are Black. And what does this mean in Hawaii anyway, more importantly, because it has been my home since 1968? Fortunately, I would not be discriminated against in Hawaii, because I clearly "pull" Caucasian. But for those who do not "pull" Caucasian, Hawaii has had a tradition of racism and classism. For example, as told in a March 2008 Honolulu Advertiser article, Hawaiian Airlines, for years after its 1929 launch, wouldn't hire local pilots, local flight attendants and local counter workers. Its discriminatory history was one of the major reasons why Aloha Airlines was founded in 1946 by Ruddy Tongg.

As we all know, one definite way to stay in control and keep a race of people down is to not loan them any money to buy a home start a business. "Bishop Bank – now First Hawaiian Bank – and Bank of Hawaii controlled the money supply and it was difficult for those without financial clout or credit to secure a loan," wrote Kelli Y. Nakamura for Densho Encyclopedia. "To address this problem, (Sakae)

Takahashi along with several Japanese Americans including former veterans, raised approximately $2 million in 1953 to establish Central Pacific Bank." After passage of Hawaii's civil rights law in 1963, the Hawaii constitutional provisions for Anti-Discrimination and Title VII in 1964, is Hawaii now the promised land as hoped for by the Rev. Martin Luther King, Jr.?

We would like to think so, but we have now been doing race discrimination cases here for the past 30 years. All races. Blacks against Caucasians. Filipinos against Blacks. Japanese against Caucasians. Hawaiians against Japanese. Samoans against Caucasians. You get the picture. This racism has permeated every sector here. The most horrific local cases have been against Blacks – the threats of lynching: The Deep South legacy of racial terror.

In the first decade of this 21st century, Charles Daniels, an African-American electrician, had worked at Lockheed Martin on the mainland and here. He reported racial harassment. Lockheed refused to discipline the harassers, but instead, retaliated against Daniels, endangering his life and setting him up for further harassment and threats by racist coworkers.

In 2008, Lockheed Martin settled the lawsuit brought by the Equal Employment Opportunity Commission (EEOC) in Hawaii for $2.5 million. The overt harassment to which Daniels was subjected while working here was some of the most severe misconduct the EEOC's Honolulu office had come across, said formed EEOC Director Timothy Riera. Sadly, in this decade another workplace terroristic death threat of being lynched is going to trial at the end of this month. The one we just filed will go to trial before the next decade. Many of our clients, especially Blacks, agonize over whether to file a complaint about harassment because of fear of retaliation. Yet many courageously stand up because they want to – they must- confront this racial terror.

There were several cases where African American's were harassed by nooses at work. Attorney Carl Varady successfully won a $ 3.8 million dollar jury verdict for an African American nurse who was discriminated against by Queen's Hospital when a photograph of a noose was placed near her locker. It is unfortunate that racist symbols used against African Americans are found in Hawaii. Hopefully these high verdicts will give notice that such racial harassment acts will be punished through large jury verdicts. See <u>Ellen Harris v. Queens Medical Center</u>, 1cc13-7001-77, Hawaii Circuit Court, Judgment 2018.

Attorney James Lewis is an attorney who is active with AALA. He primarily represents traffic matters and is known as a DUI attorney. He served as Vice President for AALA many years. He obtained his J.D. from University of Minnesota.

Attorney Eric Ferrer, African American attorney won a 2018 housing discrimination case on Maui. The jury returned a verdict of over 2.2 million dollars including attorney's fees for a disabled home owner whose home association refused reasonable accommodations and demanded that he carpet his floor because he had a wheel chair, then evicted him when he told them he needed the wood floor for his wheelchair mobility. See <u>Whites v. Villas at Kanolio Association Apt. Owners</u>, 2018 Jury judgment, Mr. Ferrer used to work with Attorney Johnnie Cochran. He now enjoys a successful practice on Maui.

Attorney Leslee Matthews worked for the City Council of Maui and then later as a Deputy Prosecutor in Maui. She enjoys her work and is very active. She graduated from the University of Hawaii Law School in 2018.

She obtained a trailblazer award from Sisters Empowering Hawaii in March 2017. She was active with the Innocent Project while she was in Law school.

Sandra Simms retired as a Judge but is still extremely active. She graduated with a J.D. from DePaul University in Chicago, Il. She was the President of the Links, Incorporated in Hawaii for several years only retiring in 2019 because she was promoted to the Western Area Committee of the Links, Inc. She was very active in mental health issues, Honolulu African American Film Festival, and Soroptomist an organization to assist women. She is a docent at the Honolulu Museum of Arts. She wrote a book entitled <u>Tales from the Bench</u> (2013, Pacific Raven Press) about her experience as a Judge in Hawaii. She is past president of AALA. She lectures at Chaminade University on the

law and is very active in the African American Community in Hawaii.
On April 2019, AALA had a new essay winner, Ms. Amira Fischer. She wrote a brilliant essay on Voting Rights Acts. She is in the 11th grade at Aiea High School. She shows much promise. Hopefully she will become an attorney and carry on the torch for African American Lawyers Association. AALA treated her at a luncheon at Little Village.

A portion of her essay follows:

The Voting Rights Act marks a watershed in the civil rights legislation in U.S. history. It was the first piece of federal legislation in the United States that prohibited racial discrimination within voting. It became the turning point for African American citizens who were now allowed the right to be given opportunities. It was the monumental movement that accelerated the process of equality for all in the United States. It didn't just grant African Americans the right to vote, but the right to be heard. It ensured that black lives did matter. The voting rights act was the start to minimizing the racial divide and an end to the unjustified legal oppression against human beings. It contributed to overcoming legal barriers that prevent African Americans from exercising the right to vote and understanding that all human beings deserve the same opportunities to make a difference. Moreover, it helped reduce racial discrimination in society. This act is so important because it became the starting point that recognized that racial discrimination inhibits the progression of society. Specifically, emphasizing that love and acceptance will go farther than hate and inequality.

This Act also wasn't only a step for Africans Americans, but actually became a breakthrough for America. This Act helped to recognize the importance of advancing our society as a whole by incorporating the potential of all citizens. It helped emphasize that America values the importance of being better and the only way to do that is to focus on helping others, not oppressing them. Ensuring voting for all no matter race represents America's values. Realization that there is no benefit to oppressing others and limiting their potential to do something great.

This Act ensured that African Americans were allowed the same political power that was granted to all American citizens. It allowed them the ability to be acknowledged no matter all the precautions taken just to take their rights away. This Act is important because it granted African Americans their fair right to now take part in the country that they live in. It allowed for their problems, feelings, and demands to be heard. They needed this voice to let others know that treating them less than human was not acceptable. It's so important that they kept trying to eliminate all injustices against them to protest that nothing is enough until it's equal. That determination contributed to the first big step was obtaining free justified political power. This allowed for African Americans to finally show others that they were people to with hopes and aspirations. They were not only just able to vote for candidates in election, but were now noticed as a prime part of the population causing candidates to appeal to the needs of African Americans. This was so important because now candidates who valued the importance of blacks and white arose helping to shape America's image and message of promoting equal opportunities for all.

AALA and BLSA dinner

AALA luncheon with Amira Fisher

NBA with AALA in Cuba

The African American Lawyers Association continues to be involved with the NAACP in Hawaii, Honolulu African American Film Festival, Martin Luther King parade and events, African American accomplishments in Hawaii.

The African American Lawyers Association was active in sponsoring films at the African American Festival, which was shown at Doris Duke Theatre. The films included "Whose Streets?" "Beale Street", "I'm Not Your Negro" which reflected problems in our judicial system. Black Lives Matters Patrice Cullors author activist and Alicia Garza appeared in Honolulu to speak about Black Lives Matters, and the need to continue the struggle to ensure African Americans are treated equally and are not killed and murdered without consequences by the police and others. Black men and women are still shot needlessly and murdered by the police and more often than not police officers are not arrested, are not indicted. When they are indicted and brought to trial, jurors, find them not guilty. Here is an article I wrote on Black lives matter. For Mahogany Magazine.

BLACK LIVES MATTER IN HAWAII

There have been recent protests in America by Black Lives Matter. The protests bring much attention to the needless unnecessary death of Black males and females by police. The latest two incidents involve a young black male named Philando Castile was stopped by a police officer for a broken tail light in Minnesota.

His girlfriend and his four year old daughter were in the car. As he reached for the identification which the police officer requested he was shot and killed right in front of his girlfriend and his four year old daughter. The girlfriend videotaped with her phone the entire incident showing that the young man did not reach for any weapon and was not a threat to the police officer. When reinforcement arrived, the police consoled the police officer who murdered this young man rather than to get medical attention. The evening before a black man named Alton Sterling, who sold music CD's out of a store in Baton Rouge, Louisiana was executed by a police officer who had him on the ground. A video tape showed that he was not resisting arrest nor reaching for any weapon. He was shot point blank four times.

The store owner who videoed the event was arrested for interfering with police officers, obstruction of justice. The police officers in both cases have not been arrested or charged for these senseless killings. In both cases the police officers were placed on paid leave, enjoying a vacation.

In solidarity with the Black Lives Matter Movement, there were protests in major cities across the country on Wednesday, July 13, 2016. In Honolulu there was a protest. Hawaii media did not write or acknowledge this protest. These photographs show approximately 40 people protested in front of the Waikiki police station against police brutality and for Black Lives Matter. Credit for the photographs goes to the World Can't Wait -Hawaii. Many of the people who protested the unnecessary killing by police of black lives are not themselves black. Anyone who sees that allowing the police to murder someone without justification is a violation of our Constitutional Right to be free.

There is pattern that police are killing African Americans and not being punished for these killings. They rarely are indicted or fired. When they are indicted, they rarely get convicted. Recently a Judge found four police officers not guilty in the death of Freddie Gray in Baltimore. Freddie Gray's neck was broken while in police custody. The officer who put Eric Garner in a choke hold, and ignored his pleas of "I can't breathe", was found not guilty in New York. Eric Garner was placed in a choke hold for selling cigarettes. The officer who choked him was not charged with a crime ie. Murder, manslaughter.

The murder of African Americans is a vestige of slavery times where many African American males in particular were killed for no good reason other than racism. They were lynched, tarred and feathered, maimed, imprisoned, hunt down, and present day are shot. The beginning of recognizing a problem is exposing it, identifying it, and remedying the problems. Thank goodness for cell phones which now record which records what happens. It is an unfortunate fact that many jurors and Judges tend to side with police over the victims of police brutality. With cell phones and videos perhaps this one sided view will stop.

The Bahamas recently issued a warning to its citizens who are traveling to the United States. The Bahamas warning states "we wish to advise all Bahamians traveling to the U.S. but especially to affected cities to exercise appropriate caution generally. In particularly young males are asked to exercise extreme caution in affected cities in their interactions with police. Do not be confrontational and cooperate."

The death of Philando Castile in Minnesota and Alton Sterling in Louisiana and Eric Garner should not be in vain. Let's look for real solutions to this ongoing problem in America and hold the police officers who engage in these killings legally responsible. This does not mean innocent police officers should be shot. The recent killings of police officers in Dallas and Baton Rouge are not justified. It is noted that the two men who shot police in Dallas and in Baton Rouge were U.S. veterans. There must be more mental health services to veterans who are trained to fight in war, but are inadequately treated for post traumatic stress and adapting to non war settings. More importantly, we must make sure all who engage in senseless killings are held accountable, not by more killings, but by enforcing equal justice in our legal system. If a police shoots someone or a citizen shoots a police officer without justification, then s/he should be disciplined, fired, stand trial, and held accountable. The police officers who killed Philando Castile in Minnesota and Alton Sterling in Louisiana have not been held accountable. The two veterans who shot at innocent police are dead. There was no trial for them. This is not equal justice.

Ahmaud Aubery was shot in the back while jogging down a public road in Georgia. It took the prosecutor several months to charge three white men with murder. Brianna Taylor was asleep in her bed in Kentucky when she was shot several times by police officers who were in the wrong house. George Floyd was killed by Minneapolis police, kneeing on his neck and crushing his body on the ground for all the world to see. Something snapped, with the exposure of George Floyd's murder, his pleas that he could not breath and the officers ignoring his pleas. The world saw, Black Lives did not matter too many times in America. Some became woke and protested, chanting

Black Lives Matter. Cities are now considering police reform and defunding police. Change is needed.

Some African Americans lawyers have left the practice of law to do other things. Karen McKinnie became a publisher of <u>Kailua Magazine</u>. Allison Jacobs became a teacher in the public schools, and a Legislative Aide. There is presently no African American Judge in Hawaii however we hope these changes in the future.

African American Lawyers Association supports reparations for slavery. Reparations for slavery are necessary to correct the evil of 250 years of slavery where African Americans built this country and contributed greatly without payment. If America should move forward it should recognize the wrong correct it with reparations. This is not a loss this is a win-win because African Americans are extremely loyal to America and will put their money back into the economy or their tax rebates. Human beings were kidnapped from Africa, brought to a different country, USA, Caribbean, sold as slaves and considered property by Courts, and laws had to work hard without pay, endured separation of families, had their language taken from them, were lynched, murdered, whipped, tortured, raped, denied their humanity all because they were Black not White. This occurred from the beginning of the founding of United States 1492 all the way up through the civil war and beyond. The vestiges of slavery continue today, discrimination, killing of African Americans by police, redlining, housing discrimination, prisons. So, when people ask why there is a need for reparations, the answer is to recognize the wrongs that have been done in the past based upon race, and to make payment because that is the only way a true apology can be accepted. Some people say well "we were not the ones who enslaved African Americans therefore we should not pay." If you are an American citizen and you profit and benefit from being an American and if you are not African American, then you are part of the system which profited from slavery. Slaves built the White House. Slaves built Washington, D.C. Slaves built most of the plantations and made America a rich strong great country but have not been recognized for this. "If you are not part of the solution you are part of the problem."

Reparations are not new. The Japanese Americans received reparations when they were wrongfully placed concentration camps in America during WWII. Jewish people received reparations because of the atrocities they went through from Germany. If someone comes and takes over your house and enslaves you, you would go to court and by using the legal process and demand justice - reparations. Reparations are positive.

There are many ways reparations can be given to African Americans who have descendants who were slaves. For example, there can be tax relief, a tax credit for African Americans and there can be tax rebates. If African Americans can establish that their ancestors worked lands then the lands can be given to them or the reasonable amount for these lands should be awarded to them with interest.

African American musicians who created music for which White musicians profited such as Elvis Presley "Hound dog", should be paid their worth in present day society. There should be an acknowledgement with payment for musical appropriation. Reparations would also show the world that America is indeed best and the greatest country because it acknowledges its wrongs and is trying to make it right. Many Banks and Insurance Companies in America became powerful and rich off of slavery, like Chase. These banks should be identified and pay African American descendants. What amount is just? This can be determined by studying the amount they profited from slavery and add interest. In some cases, reparations can be interest free loans. America should realize African Americans love this country, pay taxes, and any money they receive will go back into the American economy. It's a win-win situation.

It is important to identify who is against reparations. Very few African Americans are against reparations. The majority of people are Caucasians and some Asians who do not understand how deep race slavery history is in America. If you are new to the country you do not realize African Americans were considered second class citizens for over 500 years. It is time to wake up. It was illegal for African Americans to read or write. They did not get paid for all the work making slave owners rich. Women were raped. Consider the fact that most of the United States Presidents who owned slaves were white men. George Washington owned slaves which he did not free. Thomas Jefferson owned slaves and had several children with Sally Hemming, his slave who he did not free. There has only been one African American president and that cannot erase the racist history in America. However, reparations as a form of healing, Reparations as a form of justice can help. While it cannot undo the wrongs, it can pave the way for a better future.

AALA travelled to Cuba and Ghana with the National Bar Association. In Ghana, we distributed school books to a new school building in Kamasi, had dinner with the King of the Ashanti's, toured the slave dungeons and visited the Ghana Supreme Court.

I wrote the following about out Ghana trip which was partially published in the Hawaii State Bar Journal.

GHANA'S SLAVE DUNGEONS – SANKOFA

The world watched in July 2009 when President Barack Obama, First Lady Michelle Obama, and First Daughters Malia and Sasha went to Ghana, the first African country visited by an African-American President. While in Ghana, in addition to meeting the Ghanaian President Mills and many other dignitaries, President Obama and his family conducted a tour of the Cape Coast slave dungeon. The tour was shown on television with great detail. At the end of the tour, President Obama said "It reminds us of the capacity of human beings to commit great evil."

The National Bar Association, with Hawaii members Daphne Barbee-Wooten and Andre Wooten, went to Ghana in June 2010. Part of the tour included visiting the Cape Coast slave dungeons. When we first arrived at the Cape Coast, which is on the ocean, we met with the local chiefs who granted us permission to visit the dungeons. The chiefs also gave us bracelets as a token of friendship and poured libations for our ancestors and for a continued safe journey, before entering the slave dungeon.

The Cape Coast slave dungeon is an imposing white building which was built by the Swedes back in the 1650's to store timber. It was overtaken by the English and used as a slave port. When we first entered the slave dungeon, we held hands in a circle and sang "Lift Every Voice and Sing," commonly known as the African-American national anthem. Everyone wore white in honor of the solemn occasion of slavery's travesty and survival of Africans during the horrendous middle crossing from Africa to the Caribbean and the Americas. The oldest member of our group, 89 years old, and the youngest member of our group, 14 years old, went into the center of the circle. The 14-year-old read a poem for our ancestors remembering the sacrifice they made so that we could continue in this world. We then ventured into the first slave dungeon which was for male slaves. There we saw firsthand how our ancestors were treated as though they were pieces of property or storage. Chains still exist in the dungeon. It is cramped, musty, and dirt-filled with minimal light coming from opened slits in the walls. The tour guide was the same person who guided President Obama and his family. He explained how the slaves were captured in different parts of Ghana and taken down the river, placed in holes, and at night taken to the slave dungeons. Many stayed in the dungeons for months before the slave ships came to take them across the Atlantic Ocean and sold into slavery in the Americas and in the Caribbean. Inside the slave dungeon there were flower reefs. One of them was a Jamaican flower reef for the many ancestors who died in the dungeons. We were given candles to light for our ancestors' spirits.

We visited the female slave dungeon which was smaller than the male dungeon but just as horrific. Near the female slave dungeon was the Door of No Return. It is called the Door of No Return because once the Africans were shepherded out of the door they were thrown onto slave ships and disappeared. One the other side of the Door of No Return are rocks where present-day fisherman fish cast their nets in the blue ocean. Young men were playing soccer on the beach. Looking at the rear of the Door of No Return from the rocks you can see someone had painted the words "Door of Return" above the entrance. This was placed by visiting Jamaican dignitaries who decided to emphasize that things have changed and that people can always go back to educate themselves about the motherland and their roots. There is always a way to return from whence you came.

On the slave dungeon verandas you can see the ocean, fishing boats, and the town in the Cape Coast. Black canons with cannon balls overlook the blue sea. It is quite a contrast from the dark lightless damp dungeons below.

There is also a slave dungeon museum which we did not have time to visit. However, we were fortunate enough to visit Kofi Nyen, my sister-in-law's adopted Ghanaian son, who has an African concession stand near the Cape Coast. There we bought beads, masks, kente cloth, and other artifacts to support the Ghanaian economy.

All along the Ghanaian Coast there are many other slave dungeons which have been turned into museums. In fact, the President of Ghana, John Mills, lives in one of the slave dungeons in Accra. He converted the dungeon into a Presidential Office. This reminds me of the visit to South Africa where the newly built Constitutional Court sits. The newly built Constitutional Court was built on the old prison in Johannesburg which formerly housed President Nelson Mandela and Ghandi. Some of the cell blocks are still there on the Constitutional Court grounds. This ensures that people will never forget the travesty of slavery, wrongful imprisonment, apartheid, and to move forward as survivors in progress. This is also the meaning of Sankofa – looking back so you can move forward to improve.

THE GHANAIAN SUPREME COURT (DANCING WITH THE SUPREMES)

On June 14, 2010, the National Bar Association, including Attorney Andre Wooten and myself, visited the Ghanaian Supreme Court. The Supreme Court is located in Accra, near the Kwame Nkrumah Memorial Park and other government buildings. It is a white structure with columns. There is a court gallery upstairs and downstairs, which holds approximately 300 people. Because we were attorney observers, we sat on the first floor closest to the Supreme Court Justices. Fourteen Supreme Court Justices sat and heard oral argument from two Ghanaian attorneys. Once the Court convened, all the Justices wear wigs, which look like white floppy mops. The wigs are white or grey and do not fit on the head completely. The attorneys also have to wear these wigs along with a black gown.

Three female Supreme Court Justices and eleven male Justices were listening to the arguments. Sitting behind each Justice was a law clerk. For each male Justice there is a male law clerk and for each female Justice a female law clerk. The clerks did not have to wear wigs. There was one microphone which was passed between the Justices if they had questions of the attorneys.

The first case which was argued was whether or not to void an election to Parliament of a man who appellant argued had a British passport and therefore was not a Ghanaian citizen. The defense argued that the statute of limitations had run to contest the election and there was no proof that his client held a British passport and was not Ghanaian. After the arguments on the first case, the Supreme Court recessed and took a break. Then, the Supreme Court choir, which was located on the balcony, got up to sing. I did not understand the words of the song but it sounded like Hallelujah or a gospel singing. There were drums, tambourines and hand clapping accompanying the singing. After about 15 minutes of singing, the choir sat back down and the second argument began.

The second oral argument before the Ghanaian Supreme Court was argued by an attorney who did not wear the wig. He had a very nice afro hairstyle. The Justices immediately questioned the attorney as to why he was not properly attired. The attorney stated that his car broke down and he was unable to get his wig, which was at his house. The Judges were most upset with his appearance and stated that only because we were watching him that he was he allowed continuing his argument. His argument was never made because the Judges were also upset because he did not follow a rule which required that he specify what it is that his client was seeking. His client was in the audience and asked to stand as plaintiff. The Supreme Court Justices were very cross with this attorney who did not wear a wig and follow the rules, and indicated that they were going to dismiss his case.

The opposing counsel barely had to say anything as he had his wig and his robe on and merely agreed with what the Supreme Court

Justices had said.

After the arguments, the Supreme Court choir on the balcony stood up and began to sing again and clapped their hands. It made sense to have music in the Supreme Court to ease the tension due to serious arguments and thinking. Perhaps the United States Supreme Court will follow Ghana's lead in this matter.

After 15 minutes, the Supreme Court choir left and the Supreme Court Justices came back in without their wigs and talked about the Supreme Court of Ghana. The Chief Justice, the Honorable Georgina Wood, was educated in the Ghanaian Law School. She became the Supreme Court Chief Justice in 2007. She talked about the successful mediation program, which Ghana Supreme Court has enacted. Mediation is a short cut to the full appellate process, where the parties sit down and resolve the matter. This has greatly reduced the case load and is also a better process for the parties to resolve their problems instead of full-on lengthy and expensive litigation.

Human rights in Ghana were discussed. The Human Rights issues involved bribery and police misconduct cases.

We were invited to a reception where the Supreme Court choir once again sang songs and danced with us. In the middle of the choir, singing, clapping and dancing was Chief Justice Georgina Wood, along with other Justices; a Ghanaian television crew recorded this reception and showed it on Ghanaian television.

The Ghanaian Supreme Court Justices were very open and talked about the legal system. They said they did not have business cards because if they gave out their business cards then some people will use the cards to say they are close friends of the Justice, in order to gain an advantage. However, the Ghanaian Supreme Court has a website where cases can be read and the Justices' profile can be reviewed. In fact, on the Ghanaian website are our photographs in the photo gallery of the NBA's visit to the Supreme Court. Visiting, singing and dancing with the Supreme Court Justices of Ghana was an education opportunity to remember.

AALA continues to trail blaze and recognizing past and present achievements of African American attorneys and to ensure our legacy is not forgotten. Forward to the Future.

History List

1. First African American attorney to practice in Hawaii: T. Mc-Cants Stewart (1898)
2. First African American attorney prosecutor in Maui County, Wendall F. Crockett
3. First African American judge, Maui County: Wendall F. Crocket
   First African American professor University of Hawaii Law School, Dr. George Johnson
4. First African American female to practice law in Hawaii: Audrey F. Anderson
5. First African American female to Chair the Commission of Status of Women in Hawaii: Barbara Ratcliff
6. First African American female judge: Judge Sandra Simms
7. First President of African American Lawyers Association: William Harrison
8. First African American to sit on Hawaii Judicial Selection Commission: William Harrison
9. First African American to sit on Disciplinary Counsel Commission: Rustam A. Barbee
10. First African American working as an Assistant Federal Public Defender: Rustam A. Barbee
11. First African American female working at the State Public Defender: Daphne E. Barbee
12. First African American on the Hawaii Civil Rights Commission: Daphne E. Barbee
13. First African American to work as a EEOC Trial Attorney in Hawaii District: Daphne E. Barbee
14. First African American attorney to win a million dollar jury verdict on race discrimination in Federal Court: Andre S. Wooten
15. First African American to work in the prosecuting attorney's office: George Parker
16. First African American attorney working at the National Labor Relations Board in Honolulu: Wanda Pate

17. First African American attorney working at the National Labor Relations Board in Honolulu: Wanda Pate

18. First African American attorney working at Federal Contract Compliance Office in Honolulu: Leon Fortsen

19. First African American serving as the U.S. Attorney : Kenji Price

20. First African American scholarship winner: Sarah Bremer (1991)

21. African American Lawyers Association scholarship winners:_ Sarah Bremer (1991), Tanya McCoy, Arlandria Fields, Leah Barbee, Aaron Barbee, Kawaiarii Keaulana, Tia Gross, Arianne Harper (2006), Amira Fischer (2019).

22. Names of some of the African American attorneys who have practiced in Hawaii: T. McCants Stewart, Wendall F. Crockett, Audrey Anderson, Barbara Ratcliff, Sandra Simms, Daphne E. Barbee, Andre S. Wooten, William Harrison, Jerry I.Wilson, George Parker, Karen McKinnie, Allison Jacobs, Wanda Pate, Shana Peete, William Crockett, Leslee Matthews, Jamila Jarmon, James Lewis, Johnnie Mae Saunders, Gregory McClinton, Pamela Boyd, Khalid Mujtabaa, Solomon Johnson, Beverly Carver, James Paige, James Lewis, Eric Ferrer, Reginald Harris, Danielle Conway, Seth Harris, Francis McIntyre, Travis Stephens, Arthur Chapman, Evans Smith, Moana Crowell, Wendall Crutchfield, George Parker, Sherri Burr, Loan Schillinger, Charles Lawrence, (Prof U.H. Law School), Rustam A. Barbee, Judge Sandra Simms Ret., Shana Peete .Mark Valencia, Joseph Mottl, Karen Gibbs, Kenji Price (US Attorney) and Micah Smith (Asst. U.S. Attorney).

23. First African American law student to graduate from UH Law School, Elmer Germain.

24. Camille Nelson, 1st African American Dean at UH Law School, 2020.

CONCLUSION

There are more African American lawyers practicing law in 2009 in Hawaii than a hundred years before. Instead of two African American lawyers practicing in Hawaii in the early 1900s there are over twenty African American lawyers practicing in Hawaii in 2009. Nationwide, there is an increase in African American attorneys. An African American Attorney from Hawaii, Barack Obama, became President of the United States in 2009. Certainly more African American lawyers will follow in these footsteps. African Americans integration into Hawaiian society is still evolving. The black population has risen from barely 1% in 1900 to 3.1% in 2008. A recent Hawaii State Bar Association study showed in 2010 there were only .8 percent of African American Attorneys out of all Hawaii attorneys practicing law in Hawaii. Despite the small statistical numbers, great strides in civil rights and equality were made through the efforts of African American attorneys. Being a minority attorney in a State with the highest diverse population is not easy. At times, constant sunshine, ocean breezes and aloha spirit balances out the struggles. African American Lawyers keep marching, arguing and fighting for true equality and justice for everyone, leaving our footprints in the Hawaiian sand.

FURTHER READINGS/END NOTES

[1]Albert S. Broussard, *An African American Odyssey-The Stewarts, 1853-1963,* University of Kansas Press (1998) at page 72.

[2]12 Haw. 142 (1900)

[3]12 Haw. 329 (1900)

[4]13 Haw. 632 (1901)

[5]14 Haw. 145 (1902)

[6]Revised Statues of the Republic of Liberia, 1910-1911. *Made under the Authority of the Government of Liberia by T. McCants Stewart* (Paris: Establissements Russon,1928)

[7]12 Haw. 435, 537 (1900)

[8]323 U.S. 214 (1944)

[9]344 U.S. 483 (1954)

[10]418 U.S. 683 (1974)

[11]Interview with Douglas Crosier and Daphne Barbee-Wooten 9-12-02.

[12]Interview with Christopher Ijima and Daphne Barbee-Wooten 6-5-02.

[13]339 U.S. 629 ('1950)

[14]334 U.S. 1 (1948)

[15]334 U.S. 583 (1954)

[16]See Howard Law Journal, Vol 1 (1955), A *One, Two or Three, Which Should it Be? Conjecture on Three-Judge Court Procedure,* by Dr. Johnson.

[17]See *Dean George M. Johnson,* by Andrew E. Taslitz, The Jurist (Summer 1992) and *George Marion Johnson and the "Irrelevance of Race@,* by Peter J. Levinson, University of Hawaii Law Review, Vol.15 page1 (1993) for additional information about Dr. Johnson.

[18]The Making of a Liberal: The Autobiography of George M. Johnson (1989) at page 120.

[19]FORMAT, Michigan State University (September-October 1966),A *George M. Johnson, Jurist and Educator* by Gerald J. Keir.

[20]The Making of a Liberal: The Autobiography of George M. Johnson (1989) at page 120.

[21]See The Pacific Commercial Advertiser (December 23, 1902)

[22]See Montage: An Ethnic History of Women in Hawaii, Is the Black Woman in Hawaii? by Kay Brundage Takara (1978); Honolulu Star Bulletin, Waikiki Group has held its Ground, August 18, 1997.

[22]Interview on 6-6-03 with Barbara Ratliff and Daphne E. Barbee-Wooten.

[23]98 Haw. 358 (App. 2002)

[24]Id. At page 382.

[25]91 Haw. 405 (1999).

[26]Id. at page 414

[27]Rahsaan v. State of Hawaii, Civ. No. 00-00795 , U.S. District Court, District of Hawaii. See also The Honolulu Advertiser, *Jury backs teacher in Discrimination case* (December 5, 2002.)

[28]See African Americans in Large Law Firms: The Possible Cost of Exclusion, by Dercer, Hicke and Burke, Howard Law Journal, Vol 42 page 59 (1998), and 2000, 2005 report by ABA Commission on Racial and Ethnic Diversity in the Profession.

[29]*NAACP Demands Ouster of Judge for Racial Slur* by Mary Adamski, Honolulu Star Bulletin, March 8, 1986.

[30]Office of Civil Rights, Division IX, U.S. Dpt. Of Education, Case No. 10921017, Findings of Facts and Conclusion (July 28, 1992), and The Honolulu Advertiser, *DOE here rebuked on racial slurs* (August 17, 1992).

[31]Civ. No. 97-01038, U.S. District Court, District of Hawaii (1997); See also The Honolulu Advertiser, *Racial slur in yearbook outrages parents@* (June 28,1997) and *Yearbook claim settled for $80,000"* (August13,1998)

[32]Civ. No. 98-00797, U.S. District Court, District of Hawaii (1998)

[33]See Honolulu Advertiser, *Black Student Harassed at Iao, complaint says* (Dec. 16, 1998) and Honolulu Star Bulletin, *School racial incident stirs ouster call* (January 8,1999).

[34]World Conference Against Racism, Racial Discrimination, Xenophobia and Related Intolerance Declaration, 2001, United Nations

[35]71 Haw. 300 (1990)

[36]Id at page.302-303

[37]88 Haw.19 (1998)

[38]Smith v. MTL, Hawaii Civil Right Commission No. 92-003-PA-R-S (11-0-93)

[39]White v. State of Hawaii, University of Hawaii, Rob Wallace, Hawaii Civil Rights Commission No.97-001 PA-R, affmed in Civ. No.98-2810-06 (1st Cir.Ct.1999).

[40]State v. Hoshijo, 102 Haw. 307 (2003)

[41]2000 Census reported whites make up 92.5% of all lawyers nationwide, 3.9% are African American lawyers. African Americans, according to the 2008 Census, are 12.5% of the U.S. population.

IX APPENDIX

AFRO-AMERICAN LAWYERS ASSOCIATION
OF HAWAII

PO Box 4068
Honolulu, Hawaii 96812

ANDRE S. WOOTEN   (808) 545-4165
President   (Fax) 533-0275

RUSTAM A. BARBEE
Vice President
Treasurer

FRANCES C. MCINTYRE
Secretary

**THE STORY OF THE AFRICAN-AMERICAN LAWYERS
ASSOCIATION OF HAWAII
(AALA)**

Unfortunately, the real catalyst for the creation of AALA, was triggered by a verbal reference to "N.....s in the Wood pile", made on the bench, before television cameras, by the chief Administrative judge of the First Circuit, Felony Criminal courts in 1988.   The case involved bonds issued by Honolulu's only black bail bondsman. He was represented by an American African lawyer at the time, at a hearing involving procedural issues.

Many people commented, after this was shown on the 6 o'clock news, that this was despicable rhetoric coming from the bench; and it deprived the court proceeding of even the appearance of fairness, which is minimally necessary for substantial Due Process.

AALA went further and demanded that a black judge be appointed to the Honolulu judicial bench.   As this was really the only way to insure fairness of treatment for this historically exploited group.   Indeed lack of fair, or even token representation on the bench, may be a reason this group's numbers are over represented in the state and federal prison systems.

Largely due to AALA's vocal efforts, there is now one black female Circuit court judge and one per diem (part time) black female judge in District Court in Hawaii.   We hope to see more black judges, and at least one qualified black male, with extensive private practice experience, appointed to the bench in Hawaii in the near future.   Most judicial appointments tend to be given to government attorneys, such as former prosecutors or attorney generals, without any experience in the business side of practicing law and serving the public.

In 1989, AALA began it's CIVIL RIGHTS ESSAY SCHOLARSHIP CONTEST.   Every year since that time, it has conferred scholarship funds upon high school students, who have taken the time to write essays on diverse aspects of Civil Rights in the world today.

AALA members have served on various committees and spoken out and conducted seminars on Civil Rights and the need for full fair employment of all sectors of Hawaii's population in the judicial system, including probation officers, social workers, clerks, as well as public lawyers and judges.

As education is a key to training in these areas, AALA has regularly petitioned the Hawaii State legislature and the University of Hawaii to improve it's record of employment of Afro-American teachers and university professors, as well as the

AFRO-AMERICAN LAWYERS ASSOCIATION
OF HAWAII

PO Box 4068
Honolulu, Hawaii 96812

ANDRE S. WOOTEN   (808) 545-4165
President   (Fax) 533-0275

RUSTAM A. BARBEE
Vice President
Treasurer   THE STORY OF THE AFRICAN-AMERICAN LAWYERS
                           ASSOCIATION OF HAWAII
FRANCES C. MCINTYRE   (AALA)
Secretary

Unfortunately, the real catalyst for the creation of AALA, was triggered by a verbal reference to "N.....s in the Wood pile", made on the bench, before television cameras, by the chief Administrative judge of the First Circuit, Felony Criminal courts in 1988. The case involved bonds issued by Honolulu's only black bail bondsman. He was represented by an American African lawyer at the time, at a hearing involving procedural issues.

Many people commented, after this was shown on the 6 o'clock news, that this was despicable rhetoric coming from the bench; and it deprived the court proceeding of even the appearance of fairness, which is minimally necessary for substantial Due Process.

AALA went further and demanded that a black judge be appointed to the Honolulu judicial bench. As this was really the only way to insure fairness of treatment for this historically exploited group. Indeed lack of fair, or even token representation on the bench, may be a reason this group's numbers are over represented in the state and federal prison systems.

Largely due to AALA's vocal efforts, there is now one black female Circuit court judge and one per diem (part time) black female judge in District Court in Hawaii. We hope to see more black judges, and at least one qualified black male, with extensive private practice experience, appointed to the bench in Hawaii in the near future. Most judicial appointments tend to be given to government attorneys, such as former prosecutors or attorney generals, without any experience in the business side of practicing law and serving the public.

In 1989, AALA began it's CIVIL RIGHTS ESSAY SCHOLARSHIP CONTEST. Every year since that time, it has conferred scholarship funds upon high school students, who have taken the time to write essays on diverse aspects of Civil Rights in the world today.

AALA members have served on various committees and spoken out and conducted seminars on Civil Rights and the need for full fair employment of all sectors of Hawaii's population in the judicial system, including probation officers, social workers, clerks, as well as public lawyers and judges.

As education is a key to training in these areas, AALA has regularly petitioned the Hawaii State legislature and the University of Hawaii to improve it's record of employment of Afro-American teachers and university professors, as well as the teaching of the history of Africans before, as well as after, the trans Atlantic slavery period.

As the Hawaii State Bar Association has rejected all of AALA's prior applications for funding of it's projects, we are planning to stage a top flight jazz concert in 1996, to generate funds to create an endowment. Those funds would be used to both perpetuate the AALA Civil Rights Essay Scholarship Contest, and to hold an annual jazz concert to finance a larger scholarship effort.

There are presently approximately 50 Afro-American Lawyers in Hawaii engaged in all aspects of the legal profession.

Sincerely,

Andre' S. Wooten
Attorney At Law
AALA, President

**TESTIMONY IN SUPPORT OF A STATE HOLIDAY HONORING
DR. MARTIN LUTHER KING, JR.**

The Afro-American Lawyer's Association strongly urge this
Legislative Body to enact Martin Luther King Jr.'s birthday, the
3rd Monday in January, as a State Holiday. Dr. Martin Luther
King's contribution to the world as well as Hawaii can never be
overemphasized. Dr. King spearheaded the civil rights movement
from which many "minorities" or American people of color
benefited. Most Hawaiian residents are "minority" people.

It is important for Hawaii to recognize and celebrate the
struggle for equal rights and justice for everyone, regardless of
their race, creed, color, sex, and religious and political
beliefs. Such a holiday sends an important message to everyone
that arbitrary discrimination should be cast aside in favor of
unified sister and brotherhood.

It is curious that this State of "Aloha" with multiethnic
diversity should be opposed to having a holiday honoring Dr.
King, especially since it was the first State to ratify the
federal holiday celebrating Dr. King's birthday. By not
enacting this state holiday, a statement of opposition is in fact
made and felt. Such opposition can be construed to mean a
disagreement with the principals of equal rights for which Dr.
King fought and died for.

In response to the argument that Hawaii has too many
holidays already, such an argument overlooks the fact that Dr.
Martin Luther King's birthday is a federal holiday where no mail
is delivered, where federal banking institutions are closed,
where a majority of mainland states enjoy the holiday and
therefore do not conduct business, and where all federal offices
are closed. Therefor, only a certain amount of business can be
accomplished any way. Additionally, the surplus of State funds
last year was approximately 400 million dollars. A State holiday
would cost no more than 2% of this surplus amount. With the
holiday, there would be increased revenue through shopping, night
on the town, sales and travel to outer islands.

Celebrating the birthday of Dr. Martin Luther King will
bring pride to Hawaii as a state. To do otherwise will cause
increasing concern and negative attention from citizens all over
the world. If Hawaii wishes to live the true meaning of its
title as the Aloha State, recognition of Dr. King's birthday
is right in step with the aloha concept.

AALA TESTIMONY IN SUPPORT
OF S.B.
ESTABLISHING A PERMANENT
DR. MARTIN L. KING COMMISSION

The Afro-American Lawyers Association (AALA) strongly supports this bill , which establishes a permanent Dr. King Holiday Commission.

The past two years experience with an interim Dr. King Holiday Commission shows that good planning by dedicated individuals bring about a much needed educational awareness of civil rights in Hawaii. This past year, through the efforts of the Interim Commissioners, a great civil libertarian, Dr. James Farmer, was brought to Hawaii . Dr. Farmer gave a number of lectures on civil rights in Hawaii. The community response was overwhelming. The educational value of preserving the image and goals of Dr. King should not be underestimated. Justice and equality, for everyone is a message which can never be overstated, and this is the underlying policy which the Dr. King commission emphasizes. Without the Commission, we believe events commemorating this great African American leader will not be as well publicized and perceived. For example, before the Commission was established, the parade commemorating Dr. King was a small group of people. The parade has now grown with over 20 groups participating from all ethnic, religious and political backgrounds.

We urge your passage of this bill.

Daphne E. Barbee-Wooten
Afro-American Lawyers Association

AALA

RO-AMERICAN   LAWYERS ASSOCIATION

P.O. BOX 3448
MILILANI, HAWAII 96789-0448
(808) 523-7041

April 19, 1991

The Honorable Governor John Waihee
Executive Chambers
State Capitol
Honolulu, HI   96813

Dear Governor Waihee:

The Afro American Lawyers Association (AALA) of Hawaii urges
you to appoint an African-American lawyer Judge. Statistics show
that the prison population in Hawaii is 7% Black or African
American.   In the United States, over 50% of the male prison
population is Black or African American. Statistics also show that
race is a factor in the decision by Judges to incarcerate.   An
excellent book to read about this subject is "Black Robes-White
Justice", by Mr. Bruce Wright, a former judge in New York.   The
U.S. Census has recently reported that Hawaii has 3% African
American citizens. The percentage of African Americans is actually
higher because the military which is 1/3 African American, was not
counted as residents.   An African American Judge would enhance
Hawaii's image of a rainbow state with equal opportunity for all
races and culture.

For the past five years, two outstanding African American
lawyers have applied for judgeships. At the present time, we
endorse Attorney Sandra Simms as a judge. Attorney Simms has lived
and practiced law in Hawaii for over 10 years.   She was Justice
Hayashi's law clerk and has worked for the Corporation Council.
She has been interviewed by the Judicial Selection Commission and
has gone through their screening process.   Attorney Simms has
served on the Neighborhood Board in Mililani for 6 years, is
active in school base management (SCBM) in Mililani Uka Elementary
School, and has served on the Board of Bar Examiners for 4 years.
She is active with Hawaii Women Lawyers, and wrote an article in
"Our Rights, Our Lives" handbook which Hawaii Women Lawyers
published. Attorney Simms is active in the Afro American Lawyers
Association as our vice president and is a founding member.

Should you need further information, please contact us. We
hope you give serious consideration to our recommendation.

Sincerely,

ANDRE' S. WOOTEN, President

DAPHNE E. BARBEE-WOOTEN, Member

PAMELA D. BOYD, Secretary

JERRY I. WILSON, Member

RUSTAM A. BARBEE, Treasurer

JUDY WEIGHTMAN, Member

DSW

97 JUL -7 PM 5: 37

AFRO AMERICAN LAWYERS ASSOCIATION DANIEL K. AKAKA
WASHINGTON, D.C.
OF HAWAII
1188 Bishop Street, Suite 1909   97 JUL 14 PH 3: 27
PO Box 4068
Honolulu, Hawaii 96812

━━━━━•••••━━━━━

Andre S. Wooten   *(808) 545-4165*
President   *Fax 533-0275*

Rustam A. Barbee
Vice President
Treasurer

Karen L. McKinnie   July 1, 1997
Secretary
United States Senator Daniel Akaka
Prince Kuhio Federal Building
Room 3104
Honolulu, HI   96850

Dear Senator Akaka:

        The Hawaii African-American Lawyers' Association (AALA) is
appalled that the State of Hawaii Department of Education allowed
the Kaleheo High School yearbook to publish racially offensive
remarks pertaining to three African-American students. Enclosed
is a copy of the offensive page.

        We urge your support in condemning such racially offensive
remarks. Our President of the United States, Bill Clinton, has
recently asked the American public to engage in an honest
dialogue about racism in America. We in Hawaii can begin by
addressing the lack of racial sensitivity in our public schools.

        This is not the first time African-American students have
been targeted at Kaleheo High School. Enclosed is an article
from 1992 pertaining to remarks by a high school coach against an
African-American football player.

        The parents do not simply want an apology, they want fair
compensation because their children were singled out for racially
motivated humiliation, and they demand the Department of
Education institute, adopt and practice cultural sensitivity
training for their staff, teachers and students so that this does
not occur again. They also demand the yearbook be recalled as
this yearbook will continue to be the momento of a degrading slur
against the children. We also want the schools in Hawaii to

teach African-American history courses in the high schools, from
an African-American perspective, so that the students will have a
greater appreciation of African-American contributions in
America. We have a very deep and wonderful culture that has
survived heinous slavery and racism while contributing much to
the building of our country.

We will be happy to provide recommendations for an African-
American history curriculum within the Department of Education,
as we have done for the University of Hawaii.

Again we urge your support for racial sensitivity in our
schools and zero tolerance of ethnic and culturally derogatory
statements in these institutions.

Sincerely,

Andre ' S. Wootan
President
African-American Lawyers Association

Rustam Barbee
Vice President
African-American Lawyers Association

Karen McKinnie
Secretary
African-American Lawyers Association

encl.

cc: NAACP

AFRO AMERICAN LAWYERS ASSOCIATION OF HAWAII
1188 Bishop Street, Suite 1909 PO Box 4661
Honolulu, Hawaii 96812-4661

————————————•◦◉◦•————————————

Rustam A. Barbee
President .

Andre S. Wooten
Vice President

Daphne Barbee-Wooten
Treasurer

Frances C. McIntyre
Secretary

(808) 524-4406
Fax: 534-4306

May 24, 2000

Governor Benjamin J. Cayetano
Executive Chambers
Hawaii State Capitol
Honolulu, HI 96813

Dear Governor Cayetano:

        I write to share my concerns with you about Circuit Court Judge Sandra Simms' perceived leniency in sentencing decisions and my frustration with racial discrimination against African American students and faculty in Hawaii's public school system.

        First, according to a recent associated press article, you were critical of Judge Sandra Simms and her imposition of a 14-month prison term and probation sentence against Habib Shabazz who was convicted of sexual assault, second degree. The associated press article quoted you as stating that the sentence was "disproportionate to the crime". (See newspaper clipping enclosed). Our concern is that your comments imply that Judge Simms is "soft" on crime, when in fact, many lawyers who routinely appear before Judge Simms in criminal cases consider her to be a "tough" sentencer. I have personally represented clients in her court who have received what I consider to be substantially higher sentence than what other judges would have imposed under similar circumstances. Judge Simms is not the "mollycoddling" judge portrayed by the media as suggested in your comments. Near the same time your comments about Judge Simms were published, Judge Amano sentenced a defendant to probation in the Dana Ireland rape and murder case on the big island. I don't recall reading any negative comments from you regarding Judge Amano's sentence in that case.

        Judge Simms is the only African American Judge in Hawaii. She was appointed to the bench by your predecessor, Governor Waihee. By all accounts she possesses a keen legal mind and formerly worked as a lawyer for the City and County of Honolulu Corporation Counsel.

Governor Benjamin J. Cayetano
May 24, 2000
Page two

Significantly, I don't recall you or your office criticizing the sentencing decisions of other jurists during your administration. Indeed, I don't recall you ever commenting on Judge Del Rosario's denial of a defense mistrial motion where the prosecuting attorney inflamed the jury to convict an African American defendant by arguing that it was a mothers "worst nightmare" to come home and find "a black military guy" in bed with her daughter. (Jerome Rogan case, conviction reversed on appeal to the Hawaii Supreme Court). Frankly, your criticism against Judge Simms and your silence in the face of racist comments made in a court of law against an African American defendant begs the question of whether you pick and choose who you criticize depending upon their perceived political clout.

In order to address your concerns over disproportionate sentences, I respectfully suggest that you commission a study to analyze the sentencing patterns of all state judges to really see what sentencing patterns exist. I believe that such a study will reveal that Judge Sandra Simms is not the ultra-lenient sentencer portrayed by the media. Additionally, such a study will assist the State Judicial Selection Commission in its job when considering retention of our judges. The study could also be used to gather support for implementing appropriate sentencing guidelines to establish presumptive sentences based upon the severity of the offense and the defendant's criminal history. Sentencing guidelines will result in sentencing parity among the many judges. Adopting sentencing guidelines will also help to reduce racial sentencing disparities. (See article enclosed). The study would also ascertain whether African Americans are disproportionately sentenced to incarceration by certain judges.

Secondly, Hawaii's public schools are not friendly to African American students or faculty. African Americans comprise a small percentage of Hawaii's population. Recent events such as publishing racial slurs and a photograph of a student wearing a Ku Klux Klan outfit in the class yearbooks at Kalaheo and Castle High school, racial slurs and beatings against an African American student at Iao School, the lack of any tenured African American Professors at the University of Hawaii (UH Ethnic Studies department recently recommended that Dr. Kathryn W. Takara's teaching contract be terminated after more than 20 years of teaching at UH without tenure), Assistant UH basketball coach Rob Wallace referring to a fan as "nigger" and threatening to beat him, and UH Coach Riley Wallaces' implicit endorsement of flying the confederate flag in South Carolina, all lead to a feeling that African Americans are not welcome in Hawaii. I respectfully suggest that you begin by investigating racial discrimination in Hawaii's public schools. The disgraceful legacy of incidents at Kalaheo, Castle and Iao schools have resulted in some community leaders considering a boycott of the schools. Change needs to be implemented in our schools. The University of Hawaii has national reputation for poor performance in recruiting, hiring and retaining African American faculty. The recent treatment of Dr. Kathryn W. Takara at UH is outrageous. Unless reversed, the Ethnic Studies Department's recommendation to terminate Dr. Takara's contract will establish a low mark of shame for years to come at the University of Hawaii.

Governor Benjamin J. Cayetano
May 24, 2000
Page three

Finally, in the context of the disturbing incidents cited above, it is not surprising that many African Americans find Hawaii a hostile environment. As Governor, I suggest you exercise leadership by taking a strong public stand against racism in the courts and schools. One cannot exercise leadership through simply celebrating Dr. Martin Luther King Jr.'s holiday while proclaiming that all is well in Hawaii. To the contrary, affirmative measures are indicated. Your constituents in the Hawaii African American community are frustrated and will no longer suffer insults silently. Thank you for taking the time to consider and respond our concerns.

                              Sincerely,

Rustam A. Barbee

Andre S. Wooten

Daphne Barbee-Wooten

Frances C. McIntyre

DAPHNE E. BARBEE

ATTORNEY AT LAW

1188 BISHOP STREET, SUITE 1909, HONOLULU, HAWAII 96813
TELEPHONE (808) 533-0275

October 1, 2008

Hawaii Tourism Authority
1801 Kalakaua Avenue, 1ˢᵗ Floor
Honolulu, Hawaii 96815

TESTIMONY TO THE HAWAII TOURISM AUTHORITY
REGARDING REX JOHNSON

Dear Hawaii Tourism Authority Commissioners:

I previously wrote a letter September 12, 2008 expressing my outrage that Rex Johnson was not terminated, nor did he have the integrity to resign for receiving and forwarding on to his friends racist and sexist emails. A copy of my letter is attached to this testimony along with some of the emails, which refer to Barack Obama as a "coon" and Hilary Clinton as a "beaver", "hoe", and "bitch", photographs showing African-Americans running away from Barack Obama when he offers them jobs, and ridiculing an imaginary Black reporter telling victims of Hurricane Katrina, who are predominantly black,

> "Wazzup, mutha-fukkas! Hehr-i-cane Chamiqua be headin' fo' yo ass like Leroy on a crotch rocket! Bitch be a category fo'! So grab yo' chirren, yo' Ho, be leavin yo crib, and head fo' da nearest guv'ment office fo yo FREE shit!"

These emails are demeaning, mis-characterizes African-Americans as lazy, good-for-nothings, uses the derogatory term coon, which is synonymous with the n-word, and should not be tolerated on State computers during State time, for $200,000.00 a year. Rex Johnson's refusal to resign is an indication that he wants to drag the Hawaii Tourism Authority down with him. If he was a decent business person he would have recognized the offensive nature of the email and sent back those emails to his friends saying that he does not approve of these types of email and not to send it to him, especially on a government computer. He did not stop the emails, instead, he read them and forwarded them to his friends, reflecting his approval and use of them at the taxpayers' expense.

As a trial lawyer, I have seen many cases where employees and employers are charged with misuse of government property by using emails on government computers for personal purposes. Several people have been court martialed and prosecuted for misuse of government property (computers). The federal government prohibits federal employees from using federal computers and emails for personal purposes, and especially for racist, sexist and pornographic emails. Title VII of the Civil Rights Act prohibits racism and sexism in the workplace. Hawaii civil rights statutes, Chapter 378 HRS likewise prohibits discriminatory work environments. The Hawaii State Constitution states that every citizen should be free from discrimination on the basis of race, sex and ancestry. Hawaii State Constitution, Article 1, Section 5. See AALA Press Release, attached to this testimony.

Keeping Rex Johnson, who used State property, to receive and then forward pornography, and writings referring to Barack Obama as a "coon", Hilary Clinton as a "beaver","bitch" and "hoe", caricatures of African-Americans running away from an opportunity to have jobs, is not the type of CEO and leadership Hawaii needs for its tourist industry. He should be fired immediately, asked to pay back money for misusing State property, and a criminal investigation should begin. He should also be fined for his behavior. If he was truly sorry for receiving and forwarding these emails, he should have resigned for the better of the State and the Tourism Authority. All he really cares about is money. He has shown poor and disgusting judgment. It is interesting to note he has not stated that the email was received mistakenly or by some anonymous people. These emails were from his friends and he forwarded them on to others, thereby approving its contents. When a person accepts illegal drugs, then passes it on to friends, it is a crime. The same analogy applies to racist, sexist emails. For $200,000.00 a year, Hawaii deserves better.

Terminating Rex Johnson will show that the State of Hawaii will not tolerate these racist and sexist offensive acts by a CEO. Otherwise, HTA's image in the world market will be forever tarnished, not to mention opening itself to a civil rights lawsuit. Rex Johnson is a liability, not an asset.

Sincerely,

Daphne E. Barbee-Wooten
Attorney at Law

encl.

The Senate

RECOGNIZING
THE AFRICAN AMERICAN LAWYERS ASSOCIATION
2009 RECIPIENT OF THE
HAWAI'I FRIENDS OF CIVIL RIGHTS
DR. MARTIN LUTHER KING, JR. FRIENDS AWARDS

WHEREAS, the AFRICAN AMERICAN LAWYERS ASSOCIATION was founded in 1986 to fight for fairness and equal justice under the law for African Americans and other marginalized groups in Hawai'i;

WHEREAS, past Presidents include William A. Harrison, André S. Wooten, Sandra A. Simms, Rustam A. Barbee, and Daphne Barbee-Wooten and current President Shana Peete;

WHEREAS, the African American Lawyers Association list of accomplishments include: successfully lobbying for an African American Judge in Hawai'i, combating racism in the judicial system, participating in Martin Luther King Day events, serving on various boards and commission to ensure diversity, testifying in favor of civil rights acts, giving annual scholarships to students to encourage their participation in civil rights and law, encouraging respect for civil rights laws in honor of Thurgood Marshall, the first African American Judge of the United States Supreme Court, and T. McCants Stewart, the first black attorney in Hawai'i in 1898;

WHEREAS, the African American Lawyers Association also gives lectures on African American lawyers and civil rights law to various organizations and educational schools;

WHEREAS, the African American Lawyers Association is being recognized as a 2009 recipient of the Hawai'i Friends of Civil Rights (HFCR) Dr. Martin Luther King, Jr. Friends Awards for their outstanding contributions to Dr. Martin Luther King. Jr.'s legacy;

WHEREAS, the HFCR was established in the spring of 2007 by Faye Kennedy and Dr. Amy Agbayani to promote civil rights and the values of Dr. Martin Luther King, Jr.;

BE IT RESOLVED by the Senate of the State of Hawai'i that this body hereby honors The AFRICAN AMERICAN LAWYERS ASSOCIATION for their outstanding contributions to Dr. Martin Luther King, Jr.'s legacy.

Done this 25th day of January, 2009
State Capitol, Honolulu, Hawai'i

Clayton Hee, Sponsoring Senator

Colleen Hanabusa, President of the Senate

Carol Taniguchi, Clerk of the Senate

The 25th Legislature
Certificate No. 4

About the Author

Daphne Barbee-Wooten has authored several articles, Hawaii Bar Journal, Hawaii's First Black Lawyer, February 2004, Hawaii Bar Journal, The Lawgiver: George Marion Johnson, J.D., LLD, February 2005, Hawaii Bar Journal, "Spreading the Aloha of Civil Rights", October 1999. Hawaii Women Lawyers "Our Rights, Our Lives" hand book, contributing writer, co-editor for 3rd Edition, December 1996, Essence Magazine, African Americans in Hawaii, April 1994, Hawaii Bar Journal, "Hawaii Civil Rights Commission", August 1993, Contributing Writer in "Go Girl! The Black Woman's Guide to Travel and Adventure, "Visiting Nanny Town, (The Eight Mountain Press, 1997), "Following the Tradewinds: African Americans in Hawaii", 2004, contributing author. She also is a regular contributing writer to Mahogany and Afro-Hawaii News, monthly periodicals which emphasize events within the African American community in Hawaii. She authored "Justice for All: Selected Writings of Lloyd A. Barbee". She was President of AALA in 2003. and 2018 -2020. She is a contributing author to Black past.org, She is still a practicing attorney in Hawaii.